THE BEGINNER'S GUIDE TO Astrology

CLASS IS IN SESSION

REDFeather
MIND | BODY | SPIRIT

DUSTY BUNKER

Copyright © 2017 by Dusty Bunker

Library of Congress Control Number:
2017933989

Designed by Brenda McCallum
Cover design by Brenda McCallum

Type set in Bookmania/Book Antiqua

ISBN: 978-0-7643-5330-7
Printed in China

Published by Red Feather Mind Body Spirit
An Imprint of Schiffer Publishing, Ltd.
4880 Lower Valley Road
Atglen, PA 19310
Phone: (610) 593-1777; Fax: (610) 593-2002
E-mail: Info@schifferbooks.com
Web: www.schifferbooks.com

For our complete selection of fine books on this
and related subjects, please visit our website at
www.schifferbooks.com. You may also write for
a free catalog.

Schiffer Publishing's titles are available at special
discounts for bulk purchases for sales promotions
or premiums. Special editions, including
personalized covers, corporate imprints, and
excerpts, can be created in large quantities for
special needs. For more information, contact the
publisher.

We are always looking for people to write
books on new and related subjects. If you have
an idea for a book, please contact us at
proposals@schifferbooks.com.

DEDICATION

This book is dedicated to my students and clients,
all of whom have inspired me on this journey.

CONTENTS

ACKNOWLEDGMENTS

First I want to acknowledge Sandy Bouras. When I looked for someone to read the entire manuscript to see if it worked, I needed someone I could trust, who was intelligent, and who knows astrology. She was it. So, thank you, Sandy, for your time, the discussions, and the suggestions, like the title for this book. I love you, my friend.

Thanks go to my editor, Dinah Roseberry, who was always there to answer my questions and soothe my soul. Goddess bless editors! And to publisher Peter Schiffer. Neither of them would take no for an answer.

And thanks to my wonderful family:

To my hubby, Skip, the most perfect man in the world. He read a few chapters, although his attention does wander. But he did good. After reading him what I thought was an intense, deep, meaningful section on Saturn, there was a moment of silence as he nodded his head…then he said, "That salad was really good last night." He has four planets in sensual Taurus…what can I say?

To son, Matthew, who with his inscrutable Sagittarian wisdom, helped refine the title of this book. He also read a few chapters, offered suggestions, and approved. And he spent hours helping me work the symbols into jpegs for this manuscript. I told him he also did good, attributing it to his Sun and Mercury in the 6th house. He replied, "That's not it. I had that surgically removed."

To daughter Sarah, who also read a few chapters, even though her Mercury and Mars opposite Neptune would rather be at the lake, soaking up the music of the spheres.

To daughter April, with her Moon in Virgo in Virgo's house, who read a few chapters, and kept apologizing for marking the pages with red ink where I left out a comma or used a semi-colon incorrectly. She said she just can't help it; it glares out at her. She also approved. I sweated that one out.

And to daughter Melanie, our rock, with her Taurus Ascendant and Moon in Taurus' house, who saved me from Word frustration one memorable day, and who stored my manuscript safely, in case my computer got hungry and ate it up, or the cats decided to wrestle on my keyboard when I left my desk—it was only for a minute! She's a busy gal with two teenagers. Now she knows what I went through.

Some make "...the mistake of believing that the aim of intelligence is the expansion of knowledge rather than the depth of understanding."
—Rubicon...by Lawrence Alexander aka D. W. Buffa

DON'T LOOK AT THE NEXT PAGE . . .

I know you probably will. It's like saying don't take one of those warm chocolate chip cookies cooling on the kitchen counter; you'll burn your fingers. It's tempting, but do resist the impulse.

This illustration will only serve to confuse you at the moment. And I certainly don't want that to happen. We are going to take this journey step by step. As we do, the information on The Natural Zodiac shown will begin to fall into place. Although . . . you might want to make a copy of it, enclose it in plastic, and keep it as a helpful reference as we go through the book. Just don't peek until the times are right. Deal?

The Natural Zodiac

House 1:
Self, physical body,
one's window on the world
personal outlook on life,
health, mannerisms,
personality, new beginnings

House 2:
Personal income and security,
earning capacity
personal moveable
possessions, self-worth,
values

House 3:
Communication, how you
think, early education, local
travel, your vehicle, siblings,
neighbors, local newspapers,
libraries

House 4:
Home and family, heritage
nurturing parent
unmovable possessions,
land, domestic life

House 5:
Love, creativity, children
fun, games, gambling
entertainment, vacations
sensual enjoyments

House 6:
Your work, employees
health and healers, hygiene
medical professions
police, military, service
industry, small pets

House 7:
Relationships one-on-one
public life and social
interaction, marriage,
common law unions
partnerships, contracts

House 8:
Power, sex, money
major transformations
birth, death, inheritance
joint possessions and monies
partner's money, banks,
lotteries, insurance

House 9:
Philosophy, religion,
metaphysics, higher
education, knowledge,
publishing, foreign countries,
long journeys, the law and
the courts

House 10:
Career, public reputation
notoriety or fame,
authority figures, employer
matters outside the home

House 11:
Universal love, idealism
friends, civic groups
networking, humanitarian
enterprises, goals and
ambitions

House 12:
Wisdom, spirituality,
mysticism, selfless work
behind the scenes, places of
retreat and solitude, prisons,
hospitals, institutions

Introduction

Welcome. You are about to embark on an incredible journey, one filled with wonder and awe, insights and amazement. Astrology was the first religion of the human race. You do have to read this introduction to find out why.

But for now, let's talk about you. You are the center of the universe. Becoming aware of your centeredness brings a sense of peace and comfort. I believe the root cause of the human need for religion is the desire to belong to a greater source outside ourselves, to know that, in the vastness of this universe, we do matter. Along with the desire to connect outside ourselves, it is even more important to connect to our inner universe. First, "know thyself."

You are a reflection of what was happening in the heavens the moment you took your first breath. Because of the exact time and particular location of your birth, you take on the essence of that moment and that place. This concept of "synchronicity" was first proposed by the twentieth century Swiss psychiatrist Carl Gustav Jung, founder of analytical psychology, who wrote: "We are born at a given moment in a given place and like vintage years of wine we have the qualities of the year and of the season in which we are born. Astrology does not lay claim to anything else."

This is why a wine master, just by taste, can tell the year of a wine's harvest and the vineyard from which it came . . . the taster is keying in to the precise time and location of that wine's harvest.

Do keep in mind that your birth chart doesn't control you; you made your chart. It reveals who you are when you were born. It represents the accumulation of all that you have learned and experienced somewhere in the past. Just as a radio station sends and transmits on its own frequency, you could not have entered this life at that moment in time unless you were tuned to that precise time and that specific place.

You are unique, one of a kind, because no one can be born in the same space at the same moment that you are born—even a twin. My first astrology teacher was a twin, born minutes before his brother. Those few minutes dramatically changed their birth charts.

So remember: from your perspective, you are the center of the universe. Everything you know is around you, therefore, no one sees or experiences the world the way you do. The eighteenth century French philosopher, historian, and writer Voltaire (François-Marie Arouet), wrote that "God is a circle whose center is everywhere and circumference is nowhere."

You are that center.

Visualize a camera hovering over our solar system when you were born. Using the Earth, and specifically you *on* the Earth, as the center of the photograph, a picture is taken at the precise moment you took that first breath, a picture showing the positions of the Sun, the Moon, and the planets and how they were arranged around the Earth and around you. Therefore, from your perspective, everything in the solar system revolves around you. You stand in the middle of this solar system; you stand in the middle of the photograph which is your astrological chart.

So, you see, your astrological chart is more than a circle on a piece of paper or on your computer screen with funny squiggles scattered around a wheel. Your chart is a living representation of that moment in time and place when you were born on the earth.

Your chart is your wheel of life.

I visualize everyone walking around in the middle of their own wheel, often trying to give advice to others who walk in the middle of their own wheels. It really doesn't work. Not many people can give you truly accurate advice because they do not live in the middle of your wheel.

The one who can remotely begin to understand your perspective is an astrologer, who stands in the middle of your wheel with you, tries to shed her own perspective as much as possible, and looks out at the world the way you do. This is a sacred trust. An astrologer must always be aware that she has a duty to her clients to choose her words and the manner of describing their character and the different phases of their lives with care and optimism. No one person is omniscient; astrologers, like those in other professions, don't know everything. The astrologer must leave space for that client to work out challenges and to embrace opportunities, clearing their avenues to success. Our mantra should be: above all…do no harm.

I trust the planets. I visualize them as cosmic guardians, watching over us through the particular principles they represent. As time moves on, and the planets in your chart continue to move around your astrological wheel, around you, this movement is called "transits." The planetary transits offer you opportunities to work on those principles at specific times and in designated areas of your life.

One of my favorite lines comes from the poem *The Secret Sits* (1945) by the great American poet Robert Frost, 1874–1963: "We dance round the ring and suppose; but the Secret sits in the middle and knows." Perhaps unknowingly, he described your astrological birth chart.

We dance around the ring of our charts, interacting with life outside ourselves through love, work, our beliefs, the way we nurture and assert ourselves, the pressures we feel, and all the time the Secret sits in the middle of the chart and knows. The Secret is within you! Go within to find yourself. Be true to yourself; don't be influenced by what others think you should do or what others think you should be, if it doesn't resonate within. Tell them to stay out of your wheel!

The joy I feel in working with clients is that moment of awareness when they realize they are exactly who they should be, when they see the light . . . or the Light!

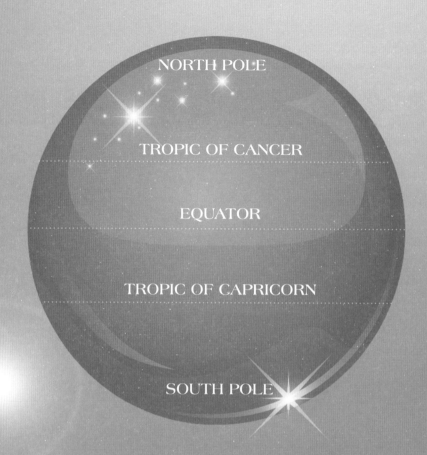

NORTH POLE

TROPIC OF CANCER

EQUATOR

TROPIC OF CAPRICORN

SOUTH POLE

Speaking of light . . .

Tropical astrology, which we are learning, is based upon the movement of the Sun over the equator between the Tropic of Cancer and the Tropic of Capricorn, which creates the seasons. This makes sense because our lives depend upon the seasons of the year.

Let's explore this a bit.

The Earth is tipped at a 23½ degree angle to the path on which it travels around the Sun. That angle never changes. So, as the Earth moves around the Sun in its yearly cycle, it receives the direct light from the Sun over only a portion of its surface. The Sun's direct light in relation to the Earth never moves above or below a belt defined by the Tropic of Cancer, 23½ degrees north of the equator, and the Tropic of Capricorn, 23½ degrees south of the equator.

At the Vernal or Spring Equinox, the sun shines directly on the equator. (Equinox means equal night; the day and night are of equal length.)

The sun's light then moves north of the equator 23½ degrees, where it stops at the Tropic of Cancer. This is the Summer Solstice (solstice means the sun is standing still).

The sun then turns to move south once again, returning to the equator, the Autumnal Equinox.

And finally, the sun's light reaches 23½ degree below the equator to the Tropic of Capricorn, the Winter Solstice, where it stands still before returning once more to the equator.

This cycle has repeated endlessly since the birth of our Mother Earth some four and one-half billion years ago.

If we were the proverbial fly on the wall, we would see the sun's repetitive movement over the equator as a serpentine flow of light between the Tropic of Cancer and the Tropic of Capricorn.

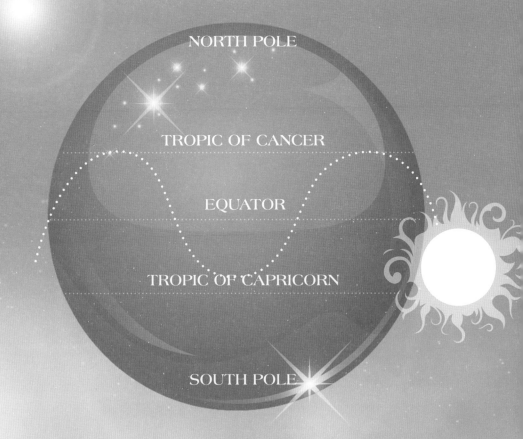

Without this permanent tip of the Earth towards the Sun, we would have no seasons; the Earth's angle to the Sun creates life as we know it. It makes sense that this undulating motion of the Sun's light over the equator has historically been portrayed as the serpent and the dragon, creatures that move in that rippling fashion. Think of all the myths and stories about serpents and dragons throughout all cultures. This same symbolism is found in the kundalini, the chi, and is the Force, as depicted in the *Star Wars* films.

These slithery symbols embody the knowledge gained from the experiences learned over the many years of our lives as the sun undulates over the equator year after year. Ultimately, the serpent became the symbol of wisdom.

Astrology was the first religion of the human race.

With the birth of human consciousness, humans sought a belief in a supernatural power that created and governed the universe and all life within it.

Imagine a world with no electricity, no villages, no shopping malls or supermarkets, just small groups of people huddled together in the dark of night for protection and eventually around campfires, looking to the star-studded heavens for answers. It must have been a wondrous and overwhelming sight; the immensity of it emphasizing how small they were in the scope of such majesty. They would naturally seek to find their place in the universe, to find meaning in their existence, to feel that they mattered.

Their first awareness, of course, was of night and day, the twenty-four-hour cycle. When the darkness descended upon them for many hours as they gathered together to wait out the night, fearful of what they could not see, they had faith that the great ball of fire would slowly lift out of the dark, shedding light on the landscape around them, providing them once again with awareness of their situation, and chasing away the fear of the unseen. They could depend upon this cycle. With the light, came awareness.

Following that, they surely became aware of the moon's cycles as it grew from darkness to light and back to darkness once again, the waxing and waning process that occurs on a lunar monthly basis. Time sprung from these observations. American Indians used to speak of time in terms of many moons ago.

Solar and Lunar eclipses must have been frightening for early people. Did the disappearance of the dependable light of the Sun portend evil happenings; did demons swallow up the sun? They would have noticed that the animals became restless and the birds ceased singing; surely time seemed suspended. When the full moon slowly disappeared into the blackness of night, their hearts must have beat faster, wondering what evil spirits stole the light from the night.

These early people observed and noted and eventually recorded the dependable movements of the sun and moon, and other celestial bodies; they noticed how the star constellations moved to different parts of the night sky depending upon the seasons.

That's when their stories began. They gave names and personal human histories to these astronomical phenomena. These became the myths that connected them with the cycles of the heavens and the earth, and gave them a position of comfort in a world over which they had little control.

As time moved on, students in the ancient mystery schools were taught the secrets of life, the secrets of the serpent symbol, embedded in the so-called four serpent signs in astrology: Aquarius, Taurus, Leo, and Scorpio. That message was to know (Aquarius), to do (Taurus), to dare (Leo), and to be silent (Scorpio).

Ancient knowledge was protected because life in those days was dangerous when one stepped outside the box of current thought. Buck the powers that be and suffer the consequences—at the least, shunned, held under house arrest, or banished, and at the worst, drowned or burned at the stake as heretics, witches, and pagans. Novices in the mystery schools learned this lesson well.

These four astrological symbols are found in the bas relief over one doorway of the Chartres Cathedral—a human (Aquarius), a bull (Taurus), a lion (Leo), and an eagle (Scorpio). They are said to represent the four apostles: Matthew, Mark, Luke, and John.

The Sphinx is said to be a composite of a human head, the body of a lion, the tail of a bull, and the wings of an eagle. (Scorpio has a number of symbols: the scorpion, the Phoenix, and the eagle, as well as the snake.)

These serpent signs—Aquarius, Taurus, Leo, and Scorpio—are fixed signs. These are the fixed forces, the glue that holds life together; they rule the middle months in each of the seasons. It's the middle months of each season that show us the self-sustaining rules we must live by, what we must hold on to, in order to survive. Without this secret knowledge put to productive use, ancient life would have been most difficult, if not impossible. The same holds true today on many levels.

As mentioned above, the serpent represents the flow of the sun over the equator, and the knowledge that the passing of days can bring us light and wisdom. We can choose to become "wise as serpents," to know that when we go out into life, we are vulnerable to the "evil" in the world; we are sheep amongst the wolves, so we need to be wise as serpents, to know when to do, when to dare, and when to be silent. We then know how to consciously lift ourselves above the negativity of life and, by example, walk the path of love, peace, and justice.

Even today, in some cultures, these wisdom seekers are seen as strange troublemakers and rebels, defying current thought patterns. Long may they live!

Let's pick up that cosmic camera once again and snap a photograph of our solar system with the Earth as the center and you directly in the middle of this picture. This is the cosmic floor plan—the geocentric view of our solar system.

Now, imagine that around the Earth are ten concentric highways—one for each of the ten planets: the Moon, the Sun, Mercury, Venus, Mars, Jupiter, Saturn, Uranus, Neptune, and Pluto. (We know the Sun is a star and the Moon is a satellite of the Earth, but we call them planets for the sake of convenience.)

Encircling these highways, beyond Pluto, is a circular blank wall around our solar system.

Imagine that every year at the exact moment the Sun's light touches the Equator going north (the Spring Equinox), it also strikes that blank wall beyond Pluto. That point on the wall is designated as zero degrees of Aries, the beginning of the Tropical Zodiac for that year.

From that point, the circular wall is divided evenly into twelve billboards, each one advertising a particular sign of the Zodiac in order: Aries, Taurus, Gemini, Cancer, Leo, Virgo, Libra, Scorpio, Sagittarius, Capricorn, Aquarius, and finally Pisces. Since every circle is 360 degrees, each sign is always 30 degrees.

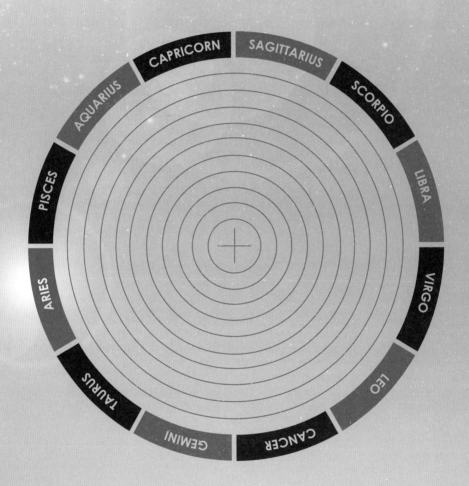

This is the Tropical Zodiac that is set up every year at the moment of the Spring Equinox when the sun is at 0 degrees of Aries.

When we travel by car, we pass billboards on the side of the highway advertising restaurants, shopping malls, car dealerships, and endless other products and enterprises that promise fulfillment for our dollar.

In the same way, from our position on Earth in the center of this wheel, imagine that we can see the ten planets traveling along their highways against the backdrop of the billboards advertising the signs of the Zodiac.

Therefore, when an astrologer looks at your chart that is constructed for the specific date and time and location of your birth, and announces that your Moon is in the sign Leo, what she means is that from our Earth-centered view, the Moon was traveling in front of the billboard advertising the sign Leo at the moment you were born. And if your Venus is in Sagittarius, that lovely planet was traveling in front of the billboard advertising Sagittarian qualities at the moment you were born. The same holds true for all the placements in your horoscope.

Once again, when you took your first breath, the cosmic camera over the Earth snapped a photograph with you as the centerpiece, at your precise location and time of birth. This photograph reveals the positions of the ten planets and the specific billboards in front of which they were traveling.

Keep in mind that your birth chart is a geocentric or earth-centered view of our solar system. We view everything in your chart from this personalized view point.

Finally, remember: you made your chart because of who you are; your chart doesn't control you. You have free will to make choices that will influence your future. Think of your chart as a spiritual bankbook with credits and debits: the debits are qualities you are here to work on; the credits are the qualities you have already developed and can spend in ways that you deem fit.

Once again, to quote the French philosopher Voltaire: "It is not more surprising to be born twice than once; everything in nature is resurrection." We are pure energy. Energy cannot be destroyed; it merely changes form.

Now, we're ready to learn astrology.

CHAPTER ONE

The Planets

Hi. I'm so glad you picked up this book because we need to talk. Let's face it . . . we're here to talk about you! Now is the time to discover that you are exactly who you are supposed to be, and not who others think you should be.

The purpose of this book is to show you the wonderful person you already are.

The first thing you need is a copy of your birth chart. If you don't have one, I will send you a free copy of your chart to use with this book. Please contact me at with your birthday, your location of birth, and the exact time of day you were born. The exact time of day is important so make an effort to find it. Before you send your e-mail request, check your data carefully to be sure it is correct, and has no typos. Include the name you want on the chart. My contact information is on page 166.

If you can't find your exact time of day of birth, even after you have dug through those crumbling cardboard boxes stored in the basement, badgered clerks at the city hall and bureau of vital statistics, contacted every family member on your fruitful family tree then, when you send for your chart, I will send you a chart set for noon on the day you were born.

I will send your chart as quickly as possible, depending upon the number of requests that land in my e-mail box on any given day. If you don't hear from me in a reasonable length of time, please check the Resource List at the back of this book for instructions on how to obtain your birth chart.

While you wait with bated breath for the magical wheel that is you, read this chapter on planets, learn the glyphs and key words for the planets, and talk to them because they are your friends. They will eventually become trusted confidants as you learn more about this fascinating subject.

But first . . . have you read the introduction? You do realize that important foundational material is often hidden in this much overlooked portion of a book. I know this because I read a book from cover to cover, in order, starting with the title page. I know . . . OCD . . . but I prefer to think of it as being extremely thorough. You need a solid foundation to support the amazing house you are about to build. Part of that solid foundation is reading the introduction.

So, for now…

I'll wait while you go back and read the introduction.

How about a little music while you read the introduction . . . hope you like Elvis Presley . . . Or maybe Beethoven's 5th. What's your pleasure?

Have you finished reading the introduction? Yes? Okay…I'm trusting you. Then let's get started.

A few pages back, I quoted a line from a character in the novel, *Rubicon*, by Lawrence Alexander: some people make "…the mistake of believing that the aim of intelligence is the expansion of knowledge rather than the depth of understanding."

This line touched me deeply. In this new Age of Aquarius where information is expanding exponentially, have we lost the ability or the desire to take the time to deeply understand any particular subject? There are books on astrology with more information than a student can take in at the beginning. With that in mind, this book is not overloaded with knowledge, but rather it leads you on the path to the depth of understanding each step in the beginning process. Be patient with yourself; take your time, and deeply understand each chapter before you go on to the next chapter.

I'm a believer in having a notebook filled with plenty of blank sheets of removable paper when learning any new subject. Please do this to prepare; you will find it helpful in making notes and drawings as we proceed.

Confucius said: "Life is really simple…but we insist on making it complicated." Keeping that in mind, you will find the instructions in this book very simple. This book is a primer. There is no need to complicate this basic study with laborious sentences and psychological nuances. Once you have mastered the basics, you can move on to the wonderful library of astrological books and perhaps classes available from other professional astrologers.

> Take your time as you go along . . . learn each section thoroughly. There is no rush. These classes were taught over many consecutive sessions.

So, fasten your seat belts; what you will learn is not only great self-therapy, but it will also open your eyes to a new world of wonder . . . and maybe even improve your relationships. That would make it worthwhile, right?

Here we go . . .

The language of astrology is composed of three basic components: the planets, the signs, and the houses. Planets represent the basic principles, signs indicate how those principles are expressed, and the houses show where those principles will act out. It is that simple.

Think of this trinity in terms of the planet (what), the sign (how), and the house (where).

PLANETS	SIGNS	HOUSES
WHAT	HOW	WHERE

To start, you will learn key words for the planets, signs, and houses; you will then be able to write simple yet accurate sentences about your planetary placements.

For example: If you have Mercury  in Scorpio in the 6th house, you would say:

I communicate (Mercury) intensely (Scorpio) at work (6th house). See the illustration below.

See how simple that is?

But first you must learn the symbols, also called the glyphs, that represent the planets and signs.

Seriously . . . as we go along, learn the symbols so they become as much a part of your consciousness as the letters of the alphabet. Remember how you learned the alphabet when you were very young. When I started school, we were taught a melody to sing along as we recited the alphabet from A to Z…which ended with: "Now I've learned my ABC's. Tell me what you think of me." We sang that for days on end in the first grade. (That was in the era before Sesame Street and the Internet.)

These astrological symbols are the language in which you will be writing, and eventually thinking. As these symbols are introduced, practice writing them on a piece of paper, and repeat them in order. Recite them in the shower or when you're baking those delicious chocolate chip cookies, or when you're driving the car or taking a walk. Or you could regale your co-workers around the water cooler with your new knowledge. We learn through repetition.

We will start with the planets.

The Order of the Planets and Their Symbols

As I mentioned in the introduction, but I will repeat it here: we know the Moon is a satellite of the earth, and Sun is a star, but for simplicity's sake, we call them planets.

Please learn the planets and their symbols in the order listed below. The Moon and the Sun are listed first, followed by Mercury, which is closest to the Sun and on out to Pluto, which is the farthest from the Sun.

The Planets

Moon

Jupiter

Sun

Saturn

Mercury

Uranus

Venus

Neptune

Mars

Pluto

(Yes, Pluto is still a planet. You can read more about that in the endnotes at the end of this book.[1])

Study this list until you can write the planets and their symbols in the order above . . . without peeking! Write them again and again until you get them right. Once again, I'll wait...

Did you do it? Remember, this is not a race. Learn each section thoroughly before proceeding. You will be glad you did.

Now that you have that information thoroughly in hand, we'll continue.

The Meaning of the Planets

The planets are your cosmic guardians, walking through life with you, constantly watching over you. They are here to instruct you concerning the basic principles that they represent. Spend time with each of them until you thoroughly understand what they have to say to you. Go to bed with them at night, listen to them in your dreams, talk with them in the morning over your bananas and yogurt and at quiet times during the day, until their purposes are second nature to you. There is no rush . . . one step at a time.

Now, take a blank piece of paper, title this page "Planets," and list the planets with their symbols down the left side of the sheet. Then, as you read the descriptions that follow, pick a few key words that describe each planet and write those words beside that planet and its symbol.

Elementary, you might say; however, there is a method to my Holmesian madness, so please follow these directions.

You will be using these planets and key words in sentences that describe you to a "T" a bit later, so be sure to do this now. Plus, there's an additional reason for these instructions, which you will discover later.

Are you with me? All right . . . let me introduce you to your cosmic guardians.

The Moon
The Principle: Emotion

The Moon embraces you protectively; don't even try to get away.

The Moon protects the Earth, like a mother hen, circling our Earth endlessly, absorbing impacts, keeping our planet tilted at the same angle to the Sun. Without the moon, the tilt of the Earth would change dramatically, eliminating the seasons. And the Earth's slight wobble would then spin wildly, turning the Earth on its side. That would spell trouble . . . just saying.

The human body reacts to the waxing and waning of the Moon. The full Moon pulls on the fluids of the Earth, including the fluids in the body. During operations under a full Moon, there are reports of more bleeding. The full Moon increases the positive ions in the air, which causes hyperactivity and unsettled human behavior. A detective friend on the local police force said that people "go crazy" under a full Moon. There are more fights and arrests. He's even seen people on the beach baying at the full Moon.

The Moon is the "X" on your life's treasure map, connecting you to that great hall of memory called the Akashic Records where everything that has ever happened to you is kept safely locked up until you need it. Your memories are stored here in your Moon, therefore, it rules your past. This nightly orb explains how you react when you don't have time to think; your reaction is instinctual based upon your past experiences.

The Moon also rules your instinctual approach to nurturing. Your childhood and the conditioning you received growing up is under the Moon's influence, as well. The Moon takes in, absorbs, stores, and nurtures you. It rules your emotions and the fluctuation of your moods. The mother and the mothering instinct come under this lunar influence as well.

This basic nurturing principle ensures that life will continue: parents protecting their young at the expense of their own lives; ferocious mother bears fighting off larger males; tiny birds amassing to attack a predator who threatens their nest. It's built into our behavior so that life will continue.

On your sheet of paper, beside the Moon and its symbol, write a few key words.

The Sun
The Principle: Identity

The Sun makes sure that, even though you run, you can't hide.

The Sun is your identity, your individuality, and your will; it is your ego and self-awareness. The Sun is not who you are when you are born; it stands for who you will become as you mature. The sign that it's in shows how you learn, through the process of individuation, to separate yourself from those around you in order to find your own identity.

You are here to make your mark as an individual, apart from those around you, through your Sun. This is your "I AM."

Just as the Sun is the fiery life-giving center of our solar system, the Sun in your chart shows how you shine, how you radiate warmth and light in your own unique way. It represents your energy, vitality, and personal strength. The Sun energizes Earth just as the Sun energizes your chart. The sign your Sun is in and the house it occupies are of key importance in your life.

At the appropriate time of year, you might lie out on your deck, or sit in the park, or visit the beach, and let the warmth of the sun soak into your body—of course, after applying lots off sunscreen lotion and avoiding 10:00 a.m. to 2:00 p.m. time periods. Appreciate how we, along with the plants and trees and wildlife, live our lives in response to the cycles of the Sun, which creates the seasons.

On your paper, beside the Sun and its symbol, make note of a few key words.

Mercury
The Principle: Communication

Mercury has a smartphone in one hand, a fitness tracker on the other wrist, and a Bluetooth wrapped around its ear.

This planet rules communication and the conscious, rational mind. It represents your ideas and your thoughts, and it allows you to process information that helps you make decisions. It also represents the thoughts that occupy your daily mind. Mercury is your conscious awareness—the operator at the central switchboard plugging in, receiving and transmitting information.

When I was a child, we had one telephone in our home mounted on the wall by the front door, and it was owned by the telephone company. Many households had only one in the entire house. How did we ever exist?

In the very early days of the phone company, rows of women wearing earphones sat at banks of switchboards that exuded hundreds of wires, connecting and disconnecting phone calls. At home, we'd pick up the phone and wait for the operator; my impatient grandfather would grab the phone and demand, "Central!" while waiting for a human voice. Yes, there were humans to take your calls.

This is your Mercury at work on a daily basis, processing all the information that comes your way. Mercury is Central, constantly directing mental traffic to the proper brain cells, so that you can think and speak coherently. It indicates your thought process.

Commonly associated with the Greek god Hermes, the messenger of the gods, Mercury rules the mind, thinking, and talking as well as messages, travelers, communication, story telling, and eloquence.

Beside Mercury and its symbol, make note of a few key words.

> Are you making notes?
> I know I'm repeating myself; it comes from years of raising four children.

Venus
The Principle: Attraction

Venus is the siren on the rocks, tempting you toward the pleasures of life.

The magnetism of Venus works through the law of attraction, seeking to create beautiful structures, be it in relationships, in art, or in pure pleasure and comfort. Venus rules love, beauty, harmony, pleasure, and money (which can buy all those beautiful things).

Through Venus, you feel drawn to another human being, although you can't always explain why. Looks may initially spark a connection, but that is brief. That other person initially fulfills a missing part of you, a part that makes you whole. Venus seeks harmonious connections through peaceful means, using her charm and magnetism to find her other half.

Venus also attracts beauty and the comforts of life, things like well-appointed homes decorated with beautiful artwork, expensive cars, and jewelry—those things that indulge the pleasure principle. And certainly foods that please the palate, artfully presented, of course. In our society, that's where the money aspect comes in.

The things that you value and the things that you love are the domain of Venus. This planet understands the value of symmetry, grace, and form; therefore, it rules all forms of refined art, including painting, sculpture, music, literature, and architecture.

But don't get her mad. You know what can happen when love is spurned or thwarted.

Beside Venus and its symbol, write a few key words

Mars
The Principle: Action

Mars bolts out of the gate before the starting pistol is fired.

Mars is pure action, your ever-ready battery. Through its sexual drive and desire, it stimulates the birth process, initiating new life in many forms—children, business, projects, ideas—but it won't hang around to see it through. That's not its job; its job is raw physical drive.

Its desire is to explore new territory, and the devil take the hindmost. It has only one direction, and that's forward. This is the warrior straining for battle, pounding its chest, screaming war chants. A frustrated Mars can lead to conflict.

Mars rules action, drive, energy, desire, passion, and competition. This planet desires to conquer on all levels, and needs outlets for its dynamic energy. In that sense, it is necessarily self-absorbed because its purpose is to spread its creative spark, to stimulate life in all its glory, so that stagnation doesn't set in. Mars moves things along.

Speaking of moving things along. My husband leads groups of first graders through the Discovery Center situated on our local Great Bay area in New Hampshire, instructing them about marine life. He evidently spent too much time at one stop because a first grade boy looked up at him and said, "Can we move on?" I guarantee that six-year-old has a strong Mars.

Beside Mars and its symbol, add a few key words.

The five previous planets are called your Personal Planets.

Jupiter
The Principle: Expansion

With Jupiter, the sky's the limit; just make sure your wings aren't made of wax.

Everything about Jupiter is big, just like the planet. Jupiter rules expansion, growth, optimism, generosity, ethics, and morality. It's these principles that help you see the bigger picture beyond your personal life. Knowledge and positive thinking are the supplies in Jupiter's backpack.

Whatever goals you set for yourself, look to Jupiter in your chart for the help you need in order to reach those higher goals. Jupiter helps you expand your horizons and urges you to reach for more. As the poet Robert Browning wrote, "Our reach should exceed our grasp, Or what's a heaven for?"

The faith of Jupiter allows you to expand beyond your personal life into society and into the wider world in order to discover how other people think and believe; it's your long distance journey to global citizenship.

Everything Jupiter touches expands: more money or over-spending and bankruptcy; spreading your beliefs or pontificating; enjoying your food or over-eating.

Confidence and success can become hubris then, like Icarus who flew too close to the Sun on wax wings, there can be falls from great heights. Whatever Jupiter does, it does in a big, big way.

Beside Jupiter and its symbol, add a few key words.

Saturn
The Principle: Contraction
Focus and Responsibility

Saturn teaches you the rules so you'll know when to break them.

To counteract Jupiter's principle of expansion—expansion without limits has popped many a colorful balloon—meet Saturn, the principle of contraction.

A good analogy here is the gestation and birth process. As the baby develops in the womb, the mother's body expands to make room for the new growth (Jupiter). At some point, when the time is right, she experiences contractions (Saturn), known as labor pains, in order to expel the baby from her body.

As the baby is born and takes its first breath, at some level, it is aware of being separated from, and alone in the world, contained within its new body with all its limitations. The moment of birth is the genesis of self-reliance. The baby must now learn to focus within the confines of its body in a world with rules and limitations.

Saturn is the teacher; it teaches you to focus. It rules structure and limits: the bones that support your body and the skin that holds it all together. It teaches you the principles of self-reliance, responsibility and discipline, and it pressures you to build a firm foundation upon which to erect your life.

Initially, Saturn points out the weaknesses in your life—the cobwebs, cracks, and leaks; it emphasizes all the rules you were taught that originally came from those authorities around you when you were growing up. Saturn embodies your fears about breaking free of those rules because, even if the rules are painful, those known perimeters provide some level of safety and comfort because you know what the boundaries are.

Eventually you begin to examine those rules for their relevancy in your life. Some are valid: boundaries, limits, and rules are necessary in a civilized society. However, other rules may need to be broken. At this point, you take responsibility, and discipline yourself to begin the process of building your own stone castle.

I call Saturn the "finger-shaker and destiny-maker." In your early years, it's always shaking its finger at you saying, "These are the rules; do this and don't do that." You may think it was your parents or whoever brought you up, those outer authorities who set the rules, but it's your selective memory that remembers those specific childhood rules. This is a deliberate process because those rules, identified by the Saturn placement in your chart, are the ones you are meant to work on in this lifetime. Your siblings will tell a different story about those childhood rules, reflecting the Saturn placement in their charts.

Saturn is the inner authority that you seek.

Beside Saturn and its symbol, add a few key words.

Jupiter and Saturn are called the Social Planets.

Uranus: *discovered 1781*
The Principle: Awakening

Uranus is that wild and crazy planet that rolls around the solar system on its side. Unpredictable, freedom loving, independent, inventive, and unconventional, this planet can turn your life upside down. And that's exactly its function: to get you out of a rut. This is the planet of surprises; you can think of 99 things that could happen, but it's the 100th that will burst from the closet and scream, "Surprise!" That will awaken you!

Not surprisingly, Uranus rules astrologers. In the minds of the more conventional, we are considered a strange, even heretical, group of people whose beliefs and practices deviate from established norms. But surprise! Astrology was the first religion. (You can find out more about that in the introduction.)

The results of Uranian events surprise everyone. It rules earthquakes and volcanic eruptions and lightning, after all, those unexpected events that shock the status quo and send people scrambling to make changes in their situations.

Uranus does the same thing in your personal life. It reveals where your rebellious side lurks, and waits for the appropriate time to upset the apple cart in order to set you on the path of positive change in your life. Uranus means to set you free from any negative restraints, to shock you into change.

The discovery of Uranus in 1781 did shock the world.

Uranus brought about the American Revolution when a ragtag band of ill-equipped American colonists took on England, the most powerful nation in the world at that time, and won. They battled for the freedom of the individual.

Also, picture Ben Franklin trotting out in a thunderstorm with a key attached to his kite in an attempt to learn more about the nature of lightning and electricity. Even if the key, the kite, and the thunderstorm are legend, Franklin proved static electricity and lightning were the same, paving the way for future developments. The fact that this story persists reinforces the connection to the discovery of Uranus.

And certainly the Industrial Revolution was a major turning point in history (1760–1840). The invention of machines took the production of materials and goods from the hand to the machine. These new technologies changed almost every aspect of daily life world wide. It truly was a revolution.

Uranus rules abrupt change, awareness, revolution, invention, independence, sudden revelations, genius, the "aha" moment.

Neptune: *discovered 1846*
The Principle: Transcendence

Neptune transcends time and space, guiding us into the realm of spirituality, imagination, creativity, idealism, compassion, mysticism, and dreams, as well as escapism, addiction, invisibility, deceit, and illusion.

Neptune transcends barriers, just as music transcends culture and language, carrying us to that "place" beyond the material world of form and structure, the world of the unconscious, where we experience visions and the divine. When we yearn for something intangible beyond this physical world, we are reaching for Neptune.

The discovery of Neptune in 1846 brought about psychoanalysis through the works of Sigmund Freud and Carl Jung, the rise of spiritualism (a few years later the Ouija board was born), the birth of the camera and films, the development of anesthesia that sends you into another world, along with a rising interest in the occult. The word "occult" comes from the Latin *occultist*; it means clandestine or hidden.

I have Neptune in my 2nd house of earning money. Early in my career, I wrote a column on dream interpretation for the *Manchester Union Leader*, the leading newspaper in New Hampshire. While recording my dreams every morning for a period of ten years, I found that I often dreamt of things before they happened. To me, déjà vu is a hazy awareness of a dream that you do not consciously recall. I believe we dream of things before they happen.

I also wrote a book called *Dream Cycles*.

Beside Neptune and its symbol, add a few key words.

Pluto: *discovered 1930*
The Principle: Transformation

With key words like sex, transformation, birth and death, renewal, power, obsession, compulsion, elimination, and control, Pluto is the heavyweight in our ring of planets. Pluto digs to the deepest levels of the hidden and dark corners of our lives and of society, and brings those elements into the light to be transformed.

Pluto rules the deepest elementary powers of human nature.

Pluto's discovery in 1930 brought with it the discovery of atomic energy, and the eventual development of weapons like the atomic bomb, capable of destruction on a massive scale.

In 1927 George Lemaitre discussed the expanding universe; in 1929 Edwin Hubble concluded from his observations that indeed the universe was expanding, which resulted in The Big Bang Theory, explaining the origin of the universe. Pluto rules "big bangs," explosions that have life-changing effects over wide ranges.

The discovery of this planet also coincided with the rise of the Nazism, and the criminal elements of the underworld. In the United States, crime was rampant and almost uncontrollable until the government finally stepped in. Once a military reservation on an isolated island in San Francisco Bay, Alcatraz became the cruelest and harshest prison in the country, feared by even the most hardened criminals. Home to 250 of the worst criminals, it became known as *Hell-catraz*. In the early years, the severe rule of silence was said to have driven some prisoners insane. Eventually the public reacted to the stories told by released prisoners, and reform began.

Pluto's discovery reached into the hidden corners of the collective unconscious, the darkest psychological forces of human nature, and pulled those negative emotions and buried histories to the surface to be recognized so that the process of transformation and healing could begin.

Pluto is raw power, transformation, and resurrection.

Beside Pluto and its symbol, add a few key words.

Phew! I need a breather after all that heavy Pluto stuff…
More Elvis?

CHAPTER TWO

The Signs

In the previous chapter, we discussed the meaning of the ten planets. Now we're going to discuss how those ten planets express themselves. We do that through the signs.

I'm going to introduce the signs a bit differently than most astrology books because I think it will be easier to learn and more fun to do it this way. I think it's a mistake to load too much information on a beginner. Rest assured, we will go into more depth about the signs in a later chapter but for now, we're going to learn the bones; we'll construct the skeleton later, and even later, we'll flesh out that skeleton. Trust me…did I say that before? . . . but I do think you will agree when we're done.

Learn the following zodiacal signs and their symbols in the order listed. You should do this now: practice writing the signs in order, along with their symbols, over and over, until they feel as natural as writing the letters of the alphabet.

Aries	Taurus	Gemini	Cancer
Leo	Virgo	Libra	Scorpio
Sagittarius	Capricorn	Aquarius	Pisces

Have you learned the signs in order, along with their symbols? If you were here in person, I would test you. But since that's not possible, I will trust that you have done so.

Now, on another piece of blank paper and from memory, write the signs in order, along with their symbols. Do this a few times until you can complete the list correctly. You know the "P" word: practice . . . practice . . . practice.

I'll wait… How about a song from Josh Groban?

All set? Then, let's move on.

Take another piece of blank paper . . . yes, another piece of paper . . . really, I know what I'm doing . . . and title that page "Signs." Beneath that, list the signs and their symbols down the left side of the paper. As you read the following descriptions, write a few key words beside each sign. Let's stick with the positive ones because, after all, you are a wonderful person.

Shortly, you will use this sheet titled "Signs," along with the one you did in Chapter 1 titled "Planets," to construct sentences about yourself.

And for your sentencing later on—hmm, that does sound ominous—maybe you should follow these instructions.

Aries: *the Ram*

As the first grader said to my husband, "Can we move on?" Aries energy is expressed dynamically and assertively. It's first, way ahead of the pack, ready to catapult into the next adventure, to explore new territory, and always compelled to be the first and best at what it does.

Aries energy is self-focused, competitive, and impulsive and, like its symbol the Ram, a male bighorn sheep, it butts heads at times. The dictionary defines "ram" as any of various devices for battering or driving, especially a battering ram, and also as a spur projecting from the bow of a warship for penetrating the hull of an enemy's ship.

A frustrated or angry Aries energy can lead to disputes and war. Ever notice the natives of this sign often have scars on their face or head? That's because they lead with their heads.

As far as this sign is concerned, there's no time for diplomacy; who has time to stand around and talk when there are mountains to climb, rivers to cross, continents to explore . . . and races to win.

Aries will get wherever it's going first, come hell or high water. There's no need to ask, "What's the rush?" because Aries is long gone before you can get the words out of your mouth. Don't even try to slow it down; it's a losing battle.

The job of Aries is the expression of fiery, adventurous, competitive, fast forward action.

On your sheet marked Signs, write a few key words for Aries.

Key Words:

Fiery

Enthusiastic

Energetic

Impulsive

Competitive

Action-oriented

Self-centered

. . . . . .

Challenging traits:

Quick-tempered

Impatient

Angry

Selfish

Taurus: *the Bull*

Key Words:

Earthy

Patient

Stable

Sensual

Loyal

Deliberate

Cautious

Practical

......

Challenging traits:

Stubborn (bull headed)

Overly possessive

Lazy

A hoarder

See that bull lazily soaking up the sun in a field of daisies. It knows there's no rush. It will move when it's good and ready, and there's not much you can do about moving it any faster, red flags or not.

When it decides to get up, it stretches, then lumbers slowly towards its goal, which most certainly has to do with its material security; you know, like a storehouse filled with food, multiple safe deposit boxes stuffed with greenbacks, and groaning closets that would shame Marcus and Neiman. (BTW: Carrie Marcus Neiman, the founder of Marcus and Neiman, was a Taurus.)

Taurus knows the value of resources and won't spend its own unnecessarily unless...it's for something it really wants. Taurus hangs on to what it owns because it's a matter of survival to these natives. To give away a possession would cause concern for its own security. You won't find it getting rid of things it might need twenty-nine years from now.

Taurus does have a hard time differentiating between "need" and "want"; to a Taurus, they are the same thing. Extremely sensual, this sign loves to fill up its senses—perfectly described in the first line of John Denver's song "You fill up my senses, like a night in the forest . . ." Taurus loves the earth, physical contact, and material things; it fills its senses through touch, smell, taste, and sound. It won't waste valuable resources foolishly.

The job of Taurus is to stabilize, secure, and learn to be a steward of the earth's bounty.

Taurus is one of the four serpent signs. (See the introduction to find out what that means.) Taurus knows what to do.

Gemini: *the Twins*

"Aren't you curious? There's a big world out there," says Gemini, who's restless and itching to get moving.

Picture the fragile butterfly, one of nature's amazing creatures that transforms from crawling on the ground as a caterpillar to dancing through the air as a butterfly wearing a rainbow of colors. It flits from flower to flower, probing for nature's sweet nectar, which is its fuel for flight. As it stops for a sweet drink at each flowering energy station, it unknowingly leaves a trail of pollen dust that stimulates the growth for all the other flowers it touches on its journey.

In the same manner, the sign Gemini's mental agility and curiosity for information scatters across many fields, leaving a trail of information that feeds and stimulates the ideas of others in their process of mental growth. Gemini's job is not to follow through on the ideas it sparks but rather to spark others into following through on the ideas it stimulates.

Gemini thirsts for variety in experience. It is quick and witty, and can charm others with its stimulating conversation. It does hop from one topic to another, so you do have to keep up. And it loves to talk, so be prepared to listen; you might get a word in sideways if you're quick enough.

Gemini's restless nature may have it job hopping as well, especially if there is not enough stimulation in its work. It's not interested in deep analysis and research, so there's no sense in trying to tie it down.

Always on the move, Gemini energy is like the celestial postman, collecting and disseminating information.

Are you writing your key words?

Key Words:

Mentally quick

Clever

Curious

Versatile

Flexible

Talkative

......

Challenging traits:

Scattered

Nervous

A chatterbox

Cancer: *the Crab*

"A rolling stone gathers no moss," says the Cancer native. "You need to settle down."

So, let's talk about crabs. An awkward segue, I agree, but... anyway. The crab has a hard outer shell and huge claws in relation to the size of its body. Observe it on the beach or inland among the leaves and trees. It never approaches its goal directly but moves obliquely this way and that. These scuttling maneuvers serve to confuse an enemy; the crab must protect its soft underbelly.

These traits can be seen in the sign Cancer, which has highly defensive instincts. Sensitive and emotional, it can retreat when necessary, but don't think it's done. It hangs in there.

Once the Cancer claws have clutched their prey, there's no getting away. Its tenacity is legendary, meant to protect the security of its young, whether it's a child or a business.

Any child of a Cancerian mother knows you'll never get away. She'll pinch your cheek, tell you you're too thin (no matter how much you weigh) and proceed to load the table with piles of home-cooked food. She'll sink to the floor to carefully place a bandage on your scuffed knee, and then shower you with so many kisses you'll forget where you hurt. She'll attend your every game, party, and award ceremony, and gather up the family in her wake. How could you possible resist her?

Cancer's need for security registers in that sugar bowl in the cupboard stuffed with rainy-day money. Home, mom, and apple pie are Cancer's trademarks.

You can forget the giant Argus with 100 eyes; mom has the all-seeing-psychic eye in the back of her head. She knows what you are doing and where you are every moment of the live-long day.

Cancer may appear passive and vulnerable but, when you rile it up, you approach at your own peril. When threatened, it can rise up to slay giants. A complex sign, Cancer experiences emotional swings, changing from sweet and childlike to warrior princess in the blink of an eye. Cancer is patriotic and loyal to home, family, and country.

Leo: *the Lion*

"You're such a stay-at-home," says Leo, "You need to get out and have some fun." Just as the Sun is the center of our solar system, Leo is the center of any gathering, shaking out its golden mane and shining its light on everyone.

Leo's job is to fire up its creative energies. Give it a stage and it will put on a *Cirque du Soleil* performance that will wow you, but Leo is adamant about being center ring where its glorious shine will delight you. Leo is the actor with the leading role, the center of attention. You'd better believe it because it will not go unnoticed. How could you ignore such magnificence?

Notice the lion in the wild, surrounded by females who do the hunting, then wait by the sidelines for him to feast first. Leo is the king after all and carries himself with great dignity.

Leo is proud, so one thing you should never ever do is step on the lion's tail; hurt its pride and the roar that resounds through the jungle has all creatures scrambling for safety.

Leo loves having fun, and has a childlike enthusiasm for games, playtime, and any creative and entertaining enterprise.

This sign radiates warmth and happiness; its positive energy infects those around it. Leo has a big heart and is willing to help you but, there is a caveat . . . you must always say "thank you." Recognition of its generous acts is essential.

This sign is bold, courageous, and will dare mighty deeds; that's why we call such a person lionhearted. Leo carries the mantle of royalty wherever it goes.

Leo is one of the four serpent signs; it dares to dare.

Key Words:

Creative

Loving

Confident

Proud

Regal

Courageous

......

Challenging traits:

Lazy

Prideful

Arrogant

Boastful

Virgo: *the Virgin*

Key Words:

Earthy

Detailed

Discriminating

Orderly

Efficient

Clean

Modest

Unassuming

......

Challenging traits:

Worrying

Overworking

Lavish spending (designer labels are essential)

Stuck in details

Modest Virgo shudders at the antics of Leo. Shunning the limelight, Virgo seeks perfection in the work it does in service to others. Kahlil Gibran, author of *The Prophet*, described the Virgo ethic perfectly: "Work is love made visible, and if you cannot work with love, it is better that you sit at the gates of the temple and take alms from those who work with joy."

Paying attention to the smallest detail, Virgo's discriminating eye does not miss a misplaced comma or a dangling participle. And the detail paid to its wardrobe has the most discriminating dressers drooling.

However, Virgo is not afraid to get down and dirty, as long as there's a hot shower available afterward. Bring an army of Virgos in after an apocalypse, and, like the remarkable earth worm in the garbage pile, they will have the mess cleaned up before you can spell "organization."

Health is very important to this sign because Virgo has to be healthy in order to work. An arsenal of medications fills the medicine cabinet, just in case. A walking-talking medical encyclopedia, Virgo knows about the rarest medical problem, and if perchance, she doesn't, she will help you dig it up.

You see, Virgo is happiest when she can roll up her sleeves and dig her hands into work: research, re-organizing, color-coding, and alphabetizing. Virgo will instruct you that your life would be so much easier and more efficient if you had things in order and placed where you can find them. That includes your office supply stock room where elastics are separated by color, your sock drawer, which should also be color-coded, and your seventy-six spices stuffed in the kitchen cabinet that should be alphabetized because then it's so much easier to find what you want, and you won't waste time that could be used more efficiently elsewhere.

Virgo does not rest on the seventh day—it's too busy organizing the world.

Libra: *the Scales*

Virgo may walk modestly in service to others but . . . you know that white line down the middle of the road? That's where Libra likes to walk. From this vantage point, it can see more clearly.

Libra continually looks at both sides in order to bring about fair and equitable solutions to situations. Libra is like the owl turning its head 270 degrees in either direction. As a result of this comprehensive view, making decisions can sometimes be difficult. However, justice and fair play are always paramount.

Libra actively seeks out relationships because the other person is the mirror through which it comes to know itself. Therefore, it is adept in public relations and in social situations. This is the charming person at the dinner party or conference engaging you in mentally stimulating conversation and then hanging on to your every word. How could you not like Libra? as Jerry Seinfeld's TV mom said about him.

Libra does want to be liked, to be accepted, and to be approved. It is aware of the psychology of human relations and is a thoughtful counselor, the one to whom you want to tell your troubles, because you feel Libra understands. Through its ability to use ideas with awareness of the other side's opinion, Libra is the ultimate peacemaker.

However, Libra at its best will never compromise what it believes to be fair and just. That's why you never push a Libra too far; it will bend just so much, although that position sometimes resembles a pretzel. The results of pushing a Libra too far can result in war.

Libra's keen sense of beauty and balance also manifests in elegant and graceful works of art.

How's that list going?

Key Words:

Justice

Peace

Cooperation

Partnerships

Harmony

Balance

Art

Beauty

......

Challenging traits:

Indecisiveness

Frustration

Anger can lead to war

Key Words:

Powerful

In control

Intense

Private

Penetrating insight

Emotionally deep

Transformative

Loyal on all levels

Psychic

......

Challenging traits:

Obsessive control

Jealousy

Revenge

Scorpio: *the Scorpion, Eagle, Phoenix, and Snake*

You won't catch Scorpio walking that white line down the middle of the road like Libra. Scorpio recognizes there's a good chance to get run over. Scorpio investigates, makes a decision, and sticks with it.

Scorpio isn't much into talking. Sometimes called the most powerful sign in the zodiac, Scorpio is silent, secretive, and intense. It most likely wrote the marriage vow "til death do us part." It is loyal to the end.

Its sexual desires run deeper than Taurus' sensuality because Scorpio seeks to investigate the magic of the sexual union and the mystery of the birth and death process. This sign defends those in its care as well as the resources needed to ensure their survival even, if necessary, unto its own death.

With highly developed instincts, Scorpio is the ultimate truth machine, able to dig deep and psychically probe beneath surfaces to penetrate the mysteries of life. It's those X-ray vision eyes that see the truth beneath the superficial constructs of life. You can almost believe this sign can, like the fabled Shaolin priest, walk through walls.

Scorpio carries a mantle of mystery and magic that makes it hard for others to truly know its depths. Its highly developed need for control is based upon its position at the doorway between life and death, those points of transition in life. It feels it has to take care of everything—with Scorpio, it's always a life and death situation—therefore, it finds it difficult to delegate responsibility to others.

I can often tell how much responsibility my female Scorpio clients bear by the size of their pocketbooks. They often carry an arsenal of weapons. If there's a problem, find the closest female with the biggest pocketbook, and she'll have something in that bottomless bag to solve your problems.

Scorpio remains silent if it cannot say exactly what it thinks or express its feelings truthfully. A powerful emotional force resides deep within this sign, reflecting in all it does.

One of the four serpent signs—I know, I'm like a dog with a bone; but please read the introduction so you will know what this means. Scorpio stores deep dark secrets.

Scorpio knows how to keep silent.

Sagittarius: *the Archer*

As opposed to Scorpio, there is no secrecy here; Sagittarius' life is an open book. It does everything in a big obvious way.

Because Sagittarius seeks truth and knowledge, it needs the freedom to explore all philosophies, societal laws, foreign lands and their cultures. Grabbing a backpack, it heads out to parts unknown; in its hurry, it's sure to forget something.

Not known for cautious thought or deliberate organization, it reacts spontaneously to the newest adventure and has faith that whatever it needs will be provided. Like the proverbial lilies of the field, it does not worry about material provisions. Although, like Christopher Columbus, it might take along the second most popular book available in fifteenth century Europe, *The Travels of Marco Polo*, to inspire it.

Sagittarius achieves its goals through the power of positive thinking. It feeds on abstract ideas, philosophies, and religious beliefs; it's concerned about the laws that maintain the well being of society as a whole.

Once Sagittarius has found the truth, as it sees it, there's no beating around the bush; you will get its unvarnished opinion. No bull horns needed. And be prepared for a lengthy sermon; this sign is not known for brevity.

Sagittarius says what it thinks even though, at times, it's unaware that it leaves a trail of crumpled bodies in its wake. It has an uncanny way of piercing the truth with its quiver of arrows.

Sagittarian insights into the thoughts of the public mind can border on prophecy, which it often shouts unashamedly from the mountaintops.

Key Words:

Outgoing

Honest

Positive

Energetic

Direct

Generous

Spontaneous

Optimistic

......

Challenging traits:

Narrow minded

Impulsive

Procrastinating

Exaggerating

Pontificating

If you don't do the key words now, you'll wish you had. Trust me.

Capricorn: *the Mountain Goat*

Key Words:

Serious

Cautious

Frugal

Hard-working

Practical

Ambitious

Security conscious

Goal oriented

......

Challenging traits:

Cold

Miserly

Stingy

Stop-at-nothing ambitious

Speaking of mountaintops, Capricorn is the sure-footed goat that climbs the highest peaks. Appalled at the casualness of Sagittarius, Capricorn's goal is to make something of itself through serious, cautious, hard work. This sign approaches life with a purpose, with a sense of obligation to achieve, to build upon the structures of the past, to reach that shining city on the hill mentioned in The Sermon on the Mount: "You are the light of the world. A city that is set on a hill cannot be hidden." Capricorn wants to reach that city and be that light. It certainly does not want to be hidden.

Capricorn believes in and will build upon the principles tested by time. Its methodical, one sure step-at-a-time approach leads to positions of authority in business, politics, and government. It takes on the mantle of leadership with ease because it believes it was destined to be there.

Capricorn has a fear of not having enough. And since it plans on hanging around for a long time—Capricorn is known as a long-lived and enduring sign—it not only builds a career but also makes sure the coffers are well stocked to ensure that it lives that long life in comfort.

Capricorn is a serious sign and dresses for success, in keeping with the trends of the day. No khakis or jeans for this native; only three-breasted suits by Gucci and Berluti dip-dyed leather oxfords.

Capricorn knows the difference between the haves and have-nots, and will use every practical, frugal, hard-working technique to become one of the former. It is the builder of cities that endure.

Aquarius: *the Water Bearer*

(Aquarius is an air sign, not a water sign. The flow from its cup represents thought waves.)

Toss Capricorn's Guccis and Berlutis. Better yet, Aquarius says, give those material items to those in need so they can make something of themselves.

Aquarius knows that one person cannot always achieve great goals alone; therefore, it seeks to work with groups in unique ways in order to achieve freedom for people from all walks of life.

Since it values independence and the freedom to speak and to think, it strives to make the world a better place by expounding those principles for others. The humanitarian, Aquarius is tolerant and idealistic, using its inventive intellect to improve worldly conditions through friends, networking, social contacts, and fund raising.

The world is Aquarius' friend; however, it cares about others in a detached manner. As the late astrologer Jeff Jawer said: "Aquarians love humanity; it's the people they have trouble with."

This sign dislikes hypocrisy and sees others as equals, regardless of their skin color, background, religious, or philosophical differences. Bring on the LGBT's.

Because Aquarius is a citizen of the world, it thinks beyond the traditional lines of thought, outside the box, so to speak . . . actually, way outside the box. Because its mind is not fettered by what other people say is the way things should be, it can explore ideas beyond the pale.

The definition of "pale" is that which is unacceptable, and "outside the agreed standards of decency." This is when Aquarius' eyes light up and its intellect kicks in. You see, this sign cares enough to investigate what those "standards of decency" are, if they make sense, and to be sure those "standards of decency" don't impede upon any one person's freedom.

Aquarius is one of the four serpent signs. It wants the truth. It knows.

Key Words:

Independent

Inventive

Tolerant

Freedom loving

Detached caring

The humanitarian

......

Challenging traits:

Stubborn

Coldly impersonal

Needlessly rebellious

Carelessly detached

Key Words:

Compassionate

Wise

Spiritual

Faithful

Imaginative

Artistic

Humorous

Sensitive

Psychic

......

Challenging
traits:

Self-pity

Timidity

Wishy-washy

Escapism

Unnecessary
martyrdom

Pisces: *the Fish*

Pisces can only shake its head at Aquarius: how can you be detached when there is so much suffering in this world?

Sensitive and compassionate, Pisces feels the hopelessness of those less fortunate. It wants nothing more than to ease the pain of the troubled masses as inscribed on the base of the Statue of Liberty: "Give me your tired, your poor, Your huddled masses yearning to breathe free, The wretched refuse of your teeming shore. Send these, the homeless, tempest-tossed, to me. I lift my lamp beside the golden door."

Pisces would rather work for the betterment of others, even under the most difficult conditions.

This sign is known as the dust pan of the Zodiac because it accumulates and absorbs the experiences and knowledge of the previous eleven signs. As a result, it contains the wisdom of the ages.

Its creative energy often expresses through gentle waves of art, quiet meditation, and/or service to the cast-offs in society, without the need for recognition. It needs no reward; its reward is in the knowing that it has contributed to the soul of the world.

With its boundless imagination and ability to picture situations in its mind, it is the perfect audience; gather a few Pisces, tell a joke, and bask in their roars of laughter.

Often tired because of its natural tendency to absorb the feelings and thoughts of others, this sign often needs to withdraw from the fast-moving pace of life to restore itself.

The wall between the material and spiritual world is porous for a Pisces. It has to live in the material world; but often slips into the world of spirit. Music soothes its soul, putting it in touch with the celestial harmonies and its spiritual home.

And there you have the twelve signs of the zodiac. Notice that the qualities of each sign are a reaction to the qualities of the previous sign. Like the ebb and flow of the tide, this process creates balance so we don't get too stuck in one type of behavior.

Change is the only constant. By observing the attitudes of each of the adjacent signs, you can see how they swing from the Yin to the Yang, reinforcing nature's dictum that, ultimately, balance is necessary for the maintenance of life.

So what I'm saying is, don't expect your mate with four planets in Cancer to get excited when you ask him to hop off on a three-month backpacking journey to the mountains of Nepal. And don't expect your child with three planets in Sagittarius and two in Gemini to settle down in the classroom.

My son has strong Sagittarius and Gemini energy in his chart. In grade school, his teachers' complaints were always that he wouldn't stay in his seat. He was always asking permission to go the boys' room or to get up and sharpen his pencils (back in the old days they actually used pencils!). Any excuse, the teachers would say, to get out of his chair. I asked him to try to modify this behavior, but I knew how difficult it was for him. Imagine me trying to explain the reason why he was so restless to his teachers!

We are who we are! I know that's redundant; however, it's true. We cannot change who we are, and the same is true of others. We can guide our children until they are adults; we can listen to our mate and friends, and offer advice when asked, but everyone stands inside her own wheel and must live her life in her own unique way. And that includes you and me.

Now, if you did make your list of the planets with the appropriate symbols and key words, you're ready to write your first sentences.

If not, please go back and do so—now it's your choice of music…

All set? Let's take a breather here. Get up and stretch; walk around the room and roll your shoulders. You deserve a break; you've worked hard. Why not rummage through the 'fridge for that chocolate bar hidden behind the celery and turnips. And you thought "out-of-sight, out-of-mind." Silly you! Take a bite.

Now that you're reenergized, why not go over this chapter, read it a few times, recognize the flow and ebb between the signs.

Once you're comfortable with the signs, settle down for the next chapter where you will write short sentences about who you are. You'll also revel in the realization that you are exactly who you should be. Promise!

CHAPTER THREE

Getting to Know Yourself

Let's get to know a little about you.

In this chapter, as you write the sentences describing your character, moments of awareness may settle into those little crevices of your mind. Your responses might be: a chuckle (yes, I do that all the time), a lift of the brow (I did that yesterday), a shake of the head (OMG, this is getting weird.)

As your life begins to unfold before your eyes, your unconscious processes of daily communication and interaction with others, shown through your planetary placements, begin to reveal your approach to life in living color.

I say "unconscious" because these traits are so ingrained in your psyche that you are unaware of them; they have been with you from the moment you took your first breath. You have been living with them all these years and will continue to do so. You become whole when, aware of these processes, you can choose to use your innate characteristics positively and constructively.

When you continually get negative responses from others because of an habitual behavior, you have the option to modify that behavior. I say "modify" because you cannot totally change your ingrained approach to life, and you shouldn't, but you can slightly alter or soften how you act so that there will be less friction in your relationships. You may even find other more productive places to express what some call your negative behavior, a place where you can "let it all hang out." I'm just saying…

Understanding how you express your characteristics as shown by your planetary placements is an eye-opening experience.

If you have the charts of family members and friends, you can try these exercises on their planetary placements as well. This is a great exercise in tolerance because you begin to see why other people are different from you. I know . . . if only everyone did things the way we do them, the world would be a better place! But give it try anyway.

By examining the charts of others, you'll find that just because your mate doesn't express his love the way you want him to, or your child has a different work ethic than what you taught her, or your pesky neighbor doesn't keep his topiary trimmed properly, they are not wrong; they are expressing themselves exactly the way they should, hopefully in a positive manner, but certainly in the manner shown by *their* planetary placements . . . not yours.

Back to you. At the end of this chapter, you may want to shake hands with your inner self as if you are meeting for the first time.

Okay . . . ready?

First, a brief primer on how to read your chart. We will use Helen's chart as an example throughout the book.

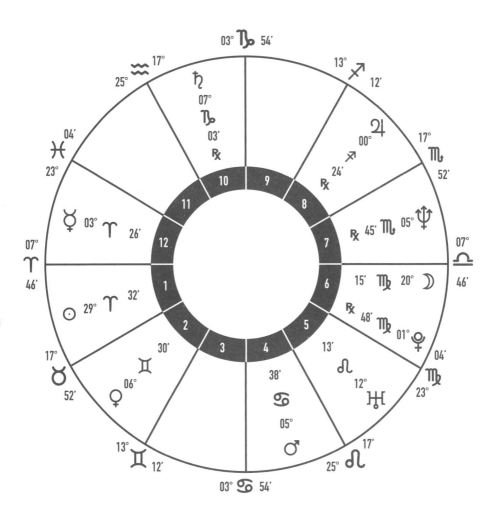

HELEN'S CHART

Do not be concerned if there are blank areas in your chart. There are ten planets spread amongst the twelve signs, so there will always be empty-looking spaces.

The Sun, Mercury, and Venus are always close to each other. (Refer to the introduction. I know; I'm persistent.) So that leaves seven other planets in various positions depending upon when you were born. Sometimes the planets are bunched together on one side of the chart; sometimes they are opposing each other; sometimes they are scattered or grouped around the wheel.

But, never fear. There are no blank spaces in your life; each segment of your wheel is covered.

Working from the outside in, you will find your planets are next to the outer ring on your wheel. There is a number beside each planet, and beyond that number is the sign that your planet is in.

Here you will work with the planet in the sign only. You may have Rs and Ds and other doodads in your chart. For now, concentrate on your planet in its sign.

In Helen's chart, you will find:

The Sun in Aries

The Moon in Virgo

Mercury in Aries

Venus in Gemini

Mars in Cancer

Jupiter in Sagittarius

Saturn in Capricorn

Uranus in Leo

Neptune in Scorpio

Pluto in Virgo

Make a list like the one above with your planets in your signs.

Then turn the page…

If you're ready to write your personal sentences, put the sheet listing the Planets and their meanings on the left, and place the sheet listing the Signs and their meanings in the middle. On the right, place a blank sheet of paper.

Now, using the key words from your Planets and Signs lists, write a short sentence about how each of your planets expresses itself through the sign in which it is placed in your chart. Find the words that feel comfortable for you.

Do this with all your planets.

Don't worry if your sentences sound stilted; they are accurate. As time goes on, the meanings will flow more smoothly, and you will discover how simple this beginning process is.

For example, in Helen's chart:

Her Moon is in Virgo:
She expresses her emotions analytically and properly.

Her Mercury is in Aries:
She speaks quickly, often without thinking first. The words seem to tumble out at breakneck speed. Her ideas can break new ground.

The following examples of planets in signs are from my files. First, I'll write a short sentence describing how the person expresses that particular principle; this will be followed by a thumbnail sketch of that individual to flesh out the short sentence. I don't expect you to write thumbnail sketches. I'm only including them to show you the accuracy of that simple sentence.

In all the examples given in this book, the names have been changed to protect the innocent. Really . . . Trust me.

The Moon
The Principle: Emotion

Moon in Taurus:
Percy expresses his emotions calmly and stably.

Thumbnail sketch:

With a Moon in Taurus, Percy instinctively expresses his emotions (Moon) calmly and stably in an unhurried manner (Taurus). Grounded and sensible (Taurus), he is a small-town banker who is trusted by the community with the town's resources. But . . . tell him to hurry because you're going to be late for the movies and see what happens! Just count to 100 and wait . . . because that's how long it will take for him to get through his preparations . . . patting his pockets for keys, wallet, and cell phone, then tucking in his shirt, buckling his belt, double knotting his shoe laces . . . do you hear someone screaming? It's probably an Aries or a Sagittarian.

· ·

Moon in Scorpio:
Mary expresses her emotions intensely and privately.

Thumbnail sketch:

With her Moon in Scorpio, Mary expresses her emotions (Moon) intensely and privately (Scorpio). She tends to remain quiet, but is stoic and strong when responding to situations that arise suddenly. Her investigative instincts run deep, down into those hidden caverns where things go bump in the night; she understands the intensity of human emotions. Mary keeps things in the vault—unlike Elaine in the Seinfield series. She is a successful and trusted sex therapist, counseling couples on their most intimate moments.

> You see how that works? Now, try this with your Moon in its sign; write a simple sentence. How does that feel?

The Sun
The Principle: Identity

Sun in Aquarius:
With his Sun in Aquarius, Ronnie is here to find his identity through independent and innovative methods.

Thumbnail sketch:

Ronnie is here to find his identity (Sun) through independent and innovative methods (Aquarius). He shines by being different, by marching to a beat only he can hear. He stands for what he believes is right and fair. As a recognized leader, even his oddity is celebrated as he strives for the principles of individual freedom (Aquarius) within his field of communication. He acts outside the box. Way out! And that's good for all of us.

Sun in Cancer:
Nancy finds her identity through protecting those in her care.

Thumbnail sketch:

With her Sun in Cancer, Nancy may appear to be meek and mild, but she is here to find her identity (Sun) through protecting (Cancer) those in her care. Like a mother hen, she stands in the background until, that is, her brood is threatened. Then watch her feathers ruffle. She is woman; she is strong. And you doubt that at your peril. When things go wrong, the room clears. Suddenly everyone has to use the bathroom or get a drink at the soda machine. Nancy shines in her work in child services, overseeing the safety of the little ones in her care.

How do you find your identity?
In what way do you shine? Write a sentence about your Sun in its sign.

Mercury
The Principle: Communication

Mercury in Libra:
James communicates in a fair and thoughtful manner.

Thumbnail sketch:

James, a lawyer with his Mercury in Libra, knows how to communicate (Mercury) with other people fairly and thoughtfully (Libra). As one who understands the psychology of relationships, he is a good listener and excellent mediator, always seeking the most equitable outcome that is fair for both sides (Libra). But he has a devil of a time deciding what shoes to wear in the morning, and where to have lunch. "You decide," he tells his wife. "No, you decide," she responds teasingly. She knows how he is. His thoughts seem consumed with making the right decisions.

Mercury in Gemini:
Mary has a curious and clever mind.

Thumbnail sketch:

Mary has a curious and clever (Gemini) mind (Mercury). She steps into every discussion with exciting new bits of information (Mercury) collected along her busy highway of experience. Witty and clever, she is adept at the art of conversation and knows how to keep the party going. You often find her in the midst of a cluster of people, dazzling them with her repartee. And then, like a wisp of wind, she's lifted off to the next stop on her conversational circuit.

What kind of communicator are you?
Write a sentence about your Mercury in its sign.

Venus
The Principle: Attraction

Venus in Pisces:
Romeo expresses his love selflessly.

Thumbnail sketch:

Romeo expresses his love (Venus) selflessly (Pisces). He is the ultimate romantic who marries only for love. Sensing the whims and feelings of his loved one, he puts her desires before his own (Pisces). He also loves working for the underprivileged in society and for all creatures, big and small (Pisces). He's been known to pick up a caterpillar from the road and gently place it in the bushes so it won't get run over.

Venus in Aquarius:
Juliet shows her love in ways that are detached but caring.

Thumbnail sketch:

Juliet shows her love (Venus) in ways that are detached but caring (Aquarius). Once, in their many years of a happy marriage, she left a note in her husband's suit pocket that said, "I love you," and once she told him he was a good husband. He, however, is a Taurus who loves to touch and feel. One day he said, "You know, hon, you never say you love me." With a puzzled look on her face, she replied, "I told you I love you the day we got married. How many times do I have to say it?" She went on to remind him of that note in his pocket three or four years ago, and not to forget the time she told him he was a good husband. That is one patient, enduring husband. Of course, he would be with a stick-to-it, hang-in-there, Moon in Taurus.

Write a sentence about how you love and what you like. No one has to know.

Mars
The Principle: Action

Mars in Leo:
Bonnie expresses her drive creatively and proudly.

Thumbnail sketch:

Bonnie expresses her drive (Mars) creatively and proudly (Leo). She loves the limelight and has the confidence of a high-paid superstar. Known as the drama queen (Mars/Leo), she can be excused for the childlike energy with which she approaches life. She uses her creative energy as a writer for children's books. What better avenue for her energy; she is the Peter Pan, eternally young and still believing in fairies.

Mars in Sagittarius:
Clyde's get-up-and-go has gone to explore fields of knowledge.

Thumbnail sketch:

Clyde's get-up-and-go (Mars) has gone to explore fields of knowledge (Sagittarius). He can't wait to "get on the road again," as the song by Willie Nelson goes. Fired up and enthusiastic (Mars), he approaches life with a thirst for adventure. With a love of outdoor sports and a curiosity about foreign cultures (Sagittarius), he couples these interests in his professional life as a tour guide for a travel company (on the road again) that offers out-of-the-way excursions. Crocodiles and boa constrictors are optional.

> How is your Mars driven? Write a sentence about your Mars in its sign.

We just finished the personal planets; now let's move on to the two social planets.

Jupiter
The Principle: Expansion

Jupiter in Aries:
Johnnie grows by asserting himself dynamically and competitively.

Thumbnail sketch:

Johnnie grows (Jupiter) by asserting himself dynamically and competitively (Aries) at whatever he chooses to do. He has yet to decide what that is but he continues to seek avenues to get there. He's spent years taking courses, expanding his knowledge (Jupiter), and exploring teaching jobs. His students love his clown-like antics in the classroom as he reenacts historical journeys (Jupiter) with over the top costumes. In the eyes of many, he has already achieved his dreams but he continues to explore the newest paths.

Jupiter in Virgo:
Gloria grows through attention to detail and her work ethic.

Thumbnail sketch:

Gloria grows (Jupiter) through attention to detail and her work ethic (Virgo). Her success is the result of her ability to gather the details (Virgo) and present her knowledge in a big way (Jupiter). She is a bigger than life (Jupiter) attorney when it comes to the finer points (Virgo) of her cases, prompting one prosecutor to state that she is a master of the details. Much of her work in the legal field is published in the local newspapers where her efforts in defending the rights of women are noted.

How will you grow this lifetime?
Your Jupiter in its sign will tell you how.

Saturn
The Principle: Contraction
Focus and Responsibility

Saturn in Libra:
Hillary's focus and responsibility in life is in mediating between opposing parties.

Thumbnail sketch:

Hillary's focus and responsibility in life (Saturn) is in mediating (Libra) between opposing parties. Born into a family of debators, discussions around the dinner table were good natured but invariably set Hillary and her brother against her mother and sister. Dad ignored them all. What she learned during meal time growing up, she has put to good use today as a respected professional who solves important crises in the field of management. She always places a tray of sweet bakery goods in the middle of the table.

Saturn in Capricorn:
Bill takes his responsibility seriously in his climb to the top.

Thumbnail sketch:

Bill takes his responsibility (Saturn) seriously in his climb to the top (Capricorn). He comes across as capable, but somewhat aloof (Capricorn). Everyone recognizes his skill, but he often gets overlooked for promotions because of his people skills. Regardless, he is focused on the pursuit of his goals in a large communications media, and he will get there, come hell or high water. He will endure . . . because he will wait out the less qualified. Saturn is patient.

Find out what Saturn expects from you by writing a sentence about your Saturn in its sign.

You might have recognized some of the anonymous names mentioned above. In all the examples throughout his book, the names have been changed to protect the innocent. I did say that earlier but, in case you don't read a book from cover to cover, I'm repeating it here. You'll find I repeat myself often. It's the mother syndrome.

Are you beginning to get the picture? Then let's move on to the Outer Planets.

Uranus, Neptune, and Pluto

The next three planets—Uranus, Neptune, and Pluto—are the outer planets. As described earlier, they were recently discovered and, because they move so slowly around the outer reaches of our solar system, they cover generations of people. Therefore, large segments of the population will have Uranus in the same sign for 7 years, Neptune in the same sign for 14 years, and Pluto in the same sign anywhere from 12–31 years. These are the periods of time that each of those three planets stay in one sign on their trips around the zodiac.

We will touch upon them briefly. Just remember, the placement of these outer planets represents your generation, and although you may not have been personally involved in the described activities, you were present and part of the whole experience; it's part of your consciousness. If one of these three outer planets does affect your birth planets or the Ascendant in your chart, you will experience their energies more personally. More about that later.

The overlapping dates below are the result of the planets' retrograde motions. All planets, except the Sun and the Moon, which we know are not planets, take different periods of time to orbit the Sun. And because their orbits are either shorter or longer than those of earth, at times, from our perspective they appear to be moving backward. We call this retrograde motion.

....

Uranus: Awakening
Spends seven years in a sign.

An example from history:
Uranus was in Taurus from 1934/1935 to 1942, awakening the need for change and innovation (Uranus) when it came to money and material resources (Taurus). Certainly our country was unsettled after the Stock Market Crash of 1929 and then the Second World War when resources were the focus. During WWII, to aid in the war effort, school children bought stamps for ten cents every Friday at school to fill their savings bonds books. To conserve resources, families kneaded yellow capsules into a white goo to make it look like butter, and grew a few vegetables in a tiny "Victory" garden, again to help the war effort.

Look at your birth chart: what sign is your Uranus in? Think about how your peers awakened to the need for change and innovation through the sign in which you find your Uranus.

Neptune: Transcendence
Spends about fourteen years in a sign.

An example from history:
Neptune was in Scorpio from 1955/1956/1957–1970, transcending the boundaries (Neptune) of traditional rules regarding sex (Scorpio). Venereal diseases spread, along with AIDs. There was a search for the spiritual meaning of life through the use of drugs as a means to escape the intensity of the world's demands.

This period initiated a new search beyond the boundaries of the physical world. In the late 1960s and into the 1970s, Maharishi Mahesh Yogi became famous as the guru to the Beatles. He was the founder of Transcendental Meditation.

Look at your birth chart: what sign is your Neptune in? Examine how your Neptune generation sought to transcend barriers in its search for the spiritual meaning of life through the sign in which it is posited.

Pluto: Transformation
Spends anywhere from twelve to thirty-one years in a sign.

An example from history:
Pluto was in Leo from 1937/1938/1939–1957, when the possibility of total annihilation, total transformation (Pluto), was possible with the explosions of the first atomic bombs. Power (Pluto) was in the hands of pompous (Leo) dictators and world leaders who expected the world to honor their superiority, the classic Divine Right of Kings (Leo).

Once again, look at your birth chart: what sign is your Pluto in? How did your Pluto generation seek transformation through the sign in which it is situated.

If you have not done so at this point, please take the first two work sheets titled Planets and Signs, that I know you have completed, and write your sentences.

Take each of your first seven planets—Moon, Sun, Mercury, Venus, Mars, Jupiter and Saturn—and describe how they behave through the signs in which they are placed. Then make a note about how the outer planets—Uranus, Neptune, and Pluto—influenced your generation.

Once you have written those brief sentences describing your first seven planets— your personal planets and your social planets—you have a partial analysis of your personality. You are beginning to know how each of these seven planets expresses itself. And you learned a little about how your peers and your generation express themselves through the outer planets Uranus, Neptune, and Pluto.

An Important Note Here about a Planet in a Sign

In old astrology and used today by some astrologers, there is a reasoning by which a planet is designated as stronger or weaker depending upon the sign in which it is placed. I don't use these assessments. If you have come across this information in the past, please disregard it for the duration of this book. When you learn more about astrology, you can make your own decision about these old assignments.

You can read why I dismiss these judgments in chapter 11, titled: The Pot of Gold. Chapter 11 also contains other astrological nuggets of important information. It's not relevant to this instructional phase, but please do read it when you're through with this class.

Just remember: your planet in its sign is exactly where it should be. It is neither good nor bad; it just is. You have choices about how you will use it.

Back to the lessons at hand. As mentioned in the first chapter, the planet represents the principle, the sign indicates how that principle is expressed, and the house shows where that principle is expressed—the trinity of the what, how, and where.

The next step is to find out where your planets express themselves, and we do that through the houses. For instance, does your Sun shine in the house of love or work or the home? Does your Mercury communicate in the house of making money or higher education or fund raising? Is your Venus hanging in the art galleries or hiding behind bathroom doors? If so, no sense in trying to cover her up . . . your chart reveals all. You might as well drop the towel.

CHAPTER FOUR
The Houses

Now it starts to get interesting! You're about to find out the meaning of the houses in which your planets took up residence when you inhaled your first breath.

The houses are those pie-shaped segments in the wheel that are numbered 1–12 counterclockwise. You will find the house numbers marked on the inner ring of your wheel.

Regardless of the movement of the planets around the astrological wheel, the houses do not move. They are stationary and their meanings never change. Again: **the houses are stationary and the meanings do not change**. Realize that everything in this world is contained within these twelve houses, obviously more than can be listed in this book.

On a personal level, each house represents a different department of your life: love, relationships, children, home, money, travel, health, career, entertainment, investments, and so forth.

So, let's take a journey around the wheel starting with the First House which begins at the left of the wheel, the house of beginnings. As you read these descriptions, feel the energy, put yourself in that position. Think about how that spark of life that is you exploded into being when you took your first breath, and how that energy spark unfolds as you move through each house. This process describes the natural unfolding of life whether it is a human being or a business or a flower.

Title a third piece of paper "Houses" and list the houses down the left side. Write a few keys words beside each house as you go along.

If you have filled in your Planets and Signs sheets as suggested in the previous chapters then, at the end of this chapter, you will be able to write complete sentences about the planetary placements in your chart.

This is way beyond exciting!

Take your time reading the following house descriptions. Feel them in your gut as you take this journey. If you truly feel this process of unfolding, you will easily remember the key words for each house.

This journey around the wheel starts from the moment of your birth and on through each stage of development: as a newborn, then as a baby, then a child, and finally into adulthood and beyond. I call this the Wheel of Life. Having a basic understanding of this life pattern, you will be able to draw upon these meanings when you describe how a planet will act in each of the houses in daily life.

Make sure that you record a few key words beside each house on your sheet titled Houses as you go along. Please pick the few that speak to you. There's a reason for this practice, which you will discover later.

Key Words:

You

Your self
awareness

Your outlook
on life

Your
appearance

How
you project
yourself

Your physical
body

Your health

New
beginnings

Self-focus

1st House:

Here you are, coming into this new life wearing just your birthday suit. No luggage in hand. Your only possession is your body, and you're not even aware of that. All you know is that there is a "you," and that you exist.

This is the point of beginnings, the moment of birth, when all you know is that you are. It's the "I am" moment, the present. There is no past; there is no future. There is just now, a point of consciousness. You have no needs and no connections to any other living being. You don't think about or want for food or human comfort or money and fame. You just *are*, totally centered on self.

This awareness is necessary so that you, as a new soul, can make the transition from one form of energy into another form of energy, which is called the birthing process. You are trying on this new consciousness, making adjustments, concentrating on fitting into your new and strange awareness.

It's as if you are a pioneer, alone in a strange land. All there is. . . is you. You need total focus on, and to be totally aware of, this new self. That's why planets in this house have the same focus on self, the need to be aware of the current moment in time, and to block out the influence of others.

The job of the first house is tunnel-vision self-awareness. This self-awareness does not imply excuses for selfishness, but rather explains and validates the need for the first house to be self-centered, self-focused.

Here, this new spark of life that is you needs to find that comfort zone in your own consciousness before you prepare to project yourself with fiery enthusiasm to discover the unexplored lands ahead, the new life you have just entered.

2nd House:

In the 1st house, you became aware that you exist. Now you're settling into your new body, trying out the arms and legs, and you realize it's too late to get out now. You're in for the long haul, so you decide to make the best of it.

In this house, you grab a travel bag to find out what's in there and hope you'll find what you're going to need to continue on this journey. Let's see. You start with the basics. You're going to need food when you're hungry . . . yup, there's a couple of jars of soft foods. Drink when you're thirsty . . . you rummage around and find little bottles of water and milk. Clothes when you're cold . . . there's a cute jumper and a pink-and-blue baby afghan. And of course, clean diapers for those . . .well, you know about those bodily functions. You know you will need these things in order to survive.

At this stage in your process, it doesn't matter who gives them to you, only that you get them. Anyway, someone does come along to hold you to her breast, and feed you when you're hungry and slate your parched throat when you're thirsty. And thank goodness, cleans your bottom when you've messed. Wow . . . that feels sooo good.

This process makes you feel good about yourself. Most importantly, you love the feeling of being held close and cooed over. You have your material needs attended to and someone who cares enough to ensure that your life will continue, therefore, you know you are valuable, that you are worth something.

You are determined to hang onto these material possessions come hell or high water. This is a house determined to hang on to what it has. After all, it's survival. Woe be to anyone who tries to pry these possessions from your tightly clenched little fists. They shouldn't even try because you will never let go. It's understandable; it's a life and death issue.

Key Words:

Your money

Your possessions

Your personal security

Moveable possessions

Your talent

Your self-worth issues

3rd House:

In the 2nd house, you learned that there are things you need in order to survive. Now, in the 3rd house, you latch on to the concept that, if what you need isn't forthcoming at the exact moment you want it, there are ways to communicate your needs.

If you're hungry or wet, a good yelling session usually brings someone running to your aid. Kicking the arms and legs, squirming, and generally twisting your body into a pretzel or straightening out like an iron rod is also quite effective. It gets results. "Hey," you think, "this is a neat way to get my message across."

You begin to notice your environment. There may be other beings in your immediate environment who are close to your size. And there are big beings who move you from place to place. You find the idea of movement exhilarating. And you like the variety of faces and places that pass before your eyes.

As you interact with these beings, you learn ways to think and express your personal point of view: is it more effective to yell and scream and generally beat your breast, or will a gurgle and a smile and a roll of your big beautiful eyes do the trick?

You do what it takes as you begin to develop your personal method of "conversation." It's exciting and liberating to finally realize that you're no longer trapped in a body where you can't get others to understand what it is you have to say.

Life in those first two houses was like that film, *Awake*, where the patient, even though he is under anesthesia, is awake and feeling everything that is going on but he can't move or scream. Well, you're awake now, and you can certainly scream.

Now that you've had plenty of practice exercising those vocal cords and you've found your voice, you'll never stop talking.

4th House:

You now recognize that the person who held you to her breast in the 2nd house, plus these other beings who seemed to hover in your vicinity in the 3rd house, form a group, a gathering of sorts, and that group is always there for you.

That one person who seems in charge and is always fussing over you is your mother (or father), the one who runs the family unit.

You feel comforted and cared for when you're in this place called home. Here your unconscious childhood patterns are reinforced, and will be the foundation for the way you set up your home in the future.

The 4th house is a place of emotional support. There are rules here because everyone contributes to the comfort, safety, and well being of the family. The screaming and tantrums don't work so well now, so you have to adjust and find your group voice, one that blends in with the voices and ideas of those in the home.

You learn to share the attention of your parents. You also learn that you must work in cooperation with the family to ensure harmonious relations.

The 4th house is your sanctuary from the vicissitudes of life, your harbor of safety, a place to which you retreat when things get rough. The rules you learn and the conditioning experienced here build the foundation of your life and set the tone for the way you will enter the world at large.

In 1865, William Ross Wallace wrote a poem titled *The Hand that Rocks the Cradle is the Hand that Rules the World*. It was written in praise of mothers as the "preeminent force for change in the world."

The 4th house is the earthly womb from which you emerge into the world of individual creative expression.

Key Words:

Home and family

Nurturing parent

Domestic and private life

Heritage

Land

Childhood patterns

Foundation of your life

Earthly womb

Environment

Key Words:

Personal
creativity

Personal love

Courtship

Children

Entertainment

Parenting
skills

Sports

Gambling

Fun

5th House:

You established your position in the family in the 4th house and you feel safe and nurtured there but . . . there's a stirring inside you; a scratch that must be itched. It's the next step in your development, and that step is the 5th house of creative self-expression.

It is now time to let your individual personality shine through. This requires that you begin to separate yourself from the family unit. You are still part of the family, but you feel the urge to express your own ideas and individual personality, your own way of acting out your creative energies.

This is the house of children and the young at heart, those who believe in possibilities. To paraphrase Thomas Edison: "Give me an uneducated man who doesn't know it can't be done, and he will go ahead and do it. But if you give me an educated man, he will give me a thousand reasons why it can't be done." This house contains your uneducated child who believes all things are possible.

Now it's recess, time for having fun that fits your particular personality. You need to explore this house of childlike curiosity and wonder, so you dash out into a creative playground. You realize that this action does require some risk. You ask yourself if it's safe to leave the family, but the overwhelming urge is to shine on your own. So you take a leap of faith and jump in with both feet.

This is the house of the Sun, so you must learn to shine on your own. You act out this new world through activities like games, sports, art, theater, writing, and generally exploring how to play.

As you grow up, you explore the fun of new romance and courtship where, once again, you take risks to find out if the other person will like the creative individual that you have become. Love and romance fill the air.

In this house, you pass your creative gifts on to your children.

6th House:

You know those games and creative projects you played at in the 5th house? In the natural order of life, you play before you work; the child inside you gets the creative juices flowing, then you take those talents into the 6th house and develop them into your skills in the work place.

The 6th house is the world of your everyday working conditions where you must interact with other employees to find your individual niche.

In the best tradition of the Wheel of Life, you should use those 5th house creative talents here in the 6th house to distinguish yourself apart from your co-workers. Here you work on perfecting your skills so that you will become an essential and recognized part of the organization; you become the craftsman.

This house defines the service you provide to your employer and the daily habits you develop, which are determined in a large measure by the job you do.

Here, you also develop routines that define your days: you get up in the morning, wash, dress, eat, and go off to work. Perhaps you work at home raising a family or running a home business. At the end of the work day, you return home or hang up your broom or shut down your computer, then eat, relax, and go to bed.

On your days off, you may revert to relaxing, perhaps reliving those childhood activities that brought you so much pleasure, in order to stay in touch with your inner child, the creative part of you.

To keep up your routine and earn your keep, you have to have a healthy body: therefore, you pay attention to your health through eating the proper foods and developing exercise regimens to keep your body fit.

If you're happy at your job—as the old saying goes—you will be too busy to be sick.

Since this is the house of small pets, dogs and cats can provide a healing presence in your life.

Key Words:

Work

Health, diet

Daily rituals

Food

Food preparation

Small pets

Clothing

Service industries

Military/ police/fire

You have spent the last six houses developing yourself in personal ways. Now it's time, in houses 7 through 12, to move beyond your personal growth and begin to interact with the outside world.

Note that houses 7 through 12 contain the same type of issues and activities as the houses 1 through 6, but instead of being acted out on a personal level, they are now acted out jointly through activities that are shared. For example: the 1st House is "me" whereas the opposite 7th House, is "me and you"; the 2nd house is *my* money, the 8th House is *our* money, and so on.

Key Words:

Balance

One-on-one relationships

Marriage

Partnerships

Contracts

Arbitrations

Public relations

Legal issues

Peace and war

7th House:

In the 1st house you were aware of just yourself. In the 7th house, you must now consider not only the 1st house of self but also the 7th house of the other. This is the house of "we," the house of relationships.

You have developed your individual personality in the first six houses, now you must reach out to others to see how they will view you, if they will accept you. In this house of relationships, being accepted and liked by other people becomes very important in your future development because it becomes necessary to work with others in order to function in the world.

Here you find out how effective you can be in personal and professional interactions one-on-one. Balance is the key. You look at both sides of any issue to find the fairest solution to any problems. You are aware that, if the other person is equally as happy as you with the agreement, then everyone wins.

Justice issues are paramount here. This is the house of partnerships, marriage, agreements, contracts, treaties, and public relations. If you are comfortable in your own skin and have developed each stage of your first six houses in harmony with who you are, you find that others like and accept you. Your relationships run smoothly and you become the mediator par excellence.

You understand how the other side functions and you present a calming influence on any unsettling relationship situations. You have the ability to soothe the savage beast.

When all else fails, there is conflict.

8th House:

The 2nd house is your money and your self-worth; the opposite 8th house is jointly held monies and shared self-worth issues.

This is the house of intense survival mode: it rules sex, birth, taxes, death, and transformation. Because you joined with another in the 7th house, you have the capability of producing new life; in the 8th house, you are now responsible for others. You join with your partner to ensure the survival of the unit, the family, the business.

Because, in our world today, joint monies are essential for the well being of the group, you protect the monies that will support the family in the future—insurance policies, investments, bank and savings accounts, and inheritances. If you have to borrow from others or use their resources to ensure the group's future survival, you now become responsible to pay off that debt.

You see the value in helping others protect their investments as well. In ancient times, the goods that were protected were food, shelter, and the actual lives of those in your care. Today, the psychological health of the group is also essential for a well-functioning society. You understand on a deep level that those who are helpless and in need of protection must feel emotionally secure within the group, the unit.

In the 2nd house, it was your self-worth issues; now the self-worth issues of the group become your responsibility, hopefully along with a partner. You want to be sure that each member of the group is well cared for, psychologically as well as materially.

The magic of birth and the mystery of death and the transformation that occurs with each of these acts of nature touch something deep inside you. Your interest puts you in touch with the magical side of life, the hidden forces of nature.

You need to understand the complexity of life and, therefore, you research these fundamental life issues.

Key Words:

Sex

Birth & death

Major transformations

Taxes

Wills

Inheritance

Partner's money

Banks

Public monies

Lotteries

Joint resources

Debt

Research

Magic

Hidden mysteries

9th House:

Now that the family, the group, is taken care of physically and psychologically through 8th house efforts, you begin to look at ways to protect them against those who would take away the goods vital to their survival.

The 3rd house is how you think; the 9th house is how we all think collectively. The 9th house rules the law and where the laws are made, the courts. Here groups gather together to pool their philosophies and ideas into cohesive rules that everyone must follow if there is to be a stable society.

The 3rd house is your individual thought process; the 9th house is the thought process of the collective mind. Single individuals become the spokespersons for these collective ideas, thus this is the house of lawyers, philosophers, teachers, and religious leaders.

Ideas and philosophies are put into writing so that worldwide audiences have access to ideas from other countries and cultures. Now we have publishers who put these ideas into print.

Ideas evolve into religious beliefs, depending upon what area of the world we look at, so the 9th house is where the development of the various religions of the world occurs. Here we search for meaning and truth.

Because the spread of ideas results in contact with other cultures, this house rules long distance and foreign travel where we are exposed to other peoples' thoughts and beliefs.

Institutions of advanced learning begin to develop around collective ideas so that higher education becomes essential to teach students who want to understand the broader world.

Since the 9th house is the house of the collective mind, in this house we find those who have the gift of prophecy. These people have the ability to tap into worldwide trends before the world becomes aware of the shifting mental patterns.

This is the house where we speak out so that others will listen, where we motivate and fire up the public consciousness so they will take action, where we seek knowledge and yearn to speak truths. This is the house of the fiery pulpit from which "truths" are spoken.

10th House:

The laws formulated in the 9th house are the foundation upon which cities are built in the 10th house.

Here we construct the buildings that represent and contain the authority of the law. They symbolize protection against chaos and anarchy. These buildings stand for years as symbols of the achievements of society.

Large businesses, churches, financial institutions, civic and government entities reside here, along with the power brokers who run them. Authority figures—the president, the monarch, the boss, the CEO, the tribal elder, the religious leader, the head of the family (the parent in charge away from home)—all live in the 10th house. These are the people who are visible to the public and who are responsible for the continuing success of the enterprise over which they have control.

The 10th house is the public home, the home away from home, in contrast to the 4th house of the personal home. In order to be successful, the leaders of these various institutions should treat their businesses or run their country with as much care as if they have the future of their personal family in their hands.

The 10th house is the top of the mountain, the one we have climbed for many years in order to achieve worldly success; it's where we think we want to be, where we find our "fifteen minutes of fame."

The 10th house is where we will be seen, where our professional ambition takes us, and where the world judges our effectiveness as a contributor to society.

The world lies heavy on these shoulders. As Lord Byron wrote in The Corsair: "Oh! If he knew the weight of splendid chains, How light the balance of his humbler pains!"

In this house, "you can run but you can't hide." Your public persona is very obvious.

Key Words:

Career

Public reputation

How the world sees you

Long term goals

Authority figures

The boss

Parent outside the home

Government institutions

11 H

Key Words:

Groups

Friends

Clubs

Organizations

Hopes

Wishes

Rewards

Humanitarian endeavors

Love beyond the personal

Adopted and step-children

11th House:

Professional expectations were met and achieved in the 10th house; we had our fifteen minutes of fame. Now we look around and say, "Is that all there is? There must be something more fulfilling we can accomplish."

In the 11th house, we begin to understand that other people may need the help we can provide from the wealth of experiences we gained in our 10th house achievements. We understand that what we were able to achieve as one individual can now be multiplied through the joining of forces with others.

We understand that the personal love and creativity we experienced through the opposite 5th house can now be translated into the 11th house of universal love and joint creative ventures.

We think about world humanity and how the environment plays a role in the hopes and wishes of other peoples and cultures. We join groups and organizations to help advance the betterment of society.

In the 5th house we took care of our children; in the 11th house we take care of other peoples' children, even if they are adults, and help them realize their dreams. In a general sense, I see this as the house of step children and adopted children.

Because our children have grown and moved on, we find love and companionship with friends who become an essential part of our lives. If our situation is such, we may find a new love in this part of our lives, a companion to share our leisure years.

We now have the resources from our years of work and achievement to enjoy more free time pursuing the things we love to do. Part of that pleasure may be helping others to achieve their goals.

Here we find people of wealth and talent who contribute their considerable resources to help those less fortunate in times of need.

12th House:

In the 11th house we contributed our resources in time or money, or both, for the betterment of the world at large; in the 12th house we get down and dirty and help scrub the floors.

The 6th house is the domain of our personal work and health; the 12th house rules universal work and universal health.

Where a Bon Jovi raises money through charitable events in order to help the needy (11th house), Mother Teresa picks a sick homeless man off the streets of Calcutta, bathes him, changes him into clean clothes, and holds him while he dies (12th house).

The 12th house is spiritual, a place where we understand that we are all one. We realize that we all came from the same source and we will all return to the same source, so that what we do for one of us, we do for all of us; everything is interconnected. "You cannot pick a flower but you disturb a star."

In the 12th, we feel the need to work for the greater good without recognition or reward. Places of solitude and confinement reside here such as retreats, reclusive religious orders, hospitals, and prisons—places that provide time for long periods of contemplation.

In this house, we go behind the scenes, sometimes voluntarily, at other times to pay a debt to society, so that we can delve into the unconscious, and search the unseen world for the wholeness of life. We examine our weaknesses . . . our skeletons and our Achilles' heels . . . as well as our strengths.

Here we yearn to touch the Divine.

We have completed the journey through the eleven houses and now we begin to understand what the "dance around the ring" is all about. We know that the next step is rebirth. Here in the 12th house, we cleanse and purify ourselves in preparation for our next turn around the Wheel of Life. As mentioned earlier, Voltaire wrote: "It is no more surprising to be born twice than to be born once."

Key Words:

Wisdom

Spirituality

Mysticism

Musical inspiration

Artistic inspiration

Compassion

Selfless work

Behind the scenes

Subconscious issues

Strengths and weaknesses

Places of solitude and rest: retreats, prisons, hospitals

The Houses are reprinted with permission from *Dell Horoscope Magazine, The Wheel of Life*, by dusty bunker in the May 2010 issue.

And there you have it…this wonderful Wheel of Life.

Did you feel the process? You might want to take this journey more than once.

The astrological Wheel of Life begins with your first breath, at the beginning point in the 1st house, and continues around the wheel counter-clockwise through all the experiences of the other houses until it empties into the spiritual 12th house. It is in the 12th house that those experiences are absorbed into the sea of wisdom in preparation for a new cycle.

This incredible journey around the wheel is every individual's psychological pattern of growth and development. It also corresponds to the birth and development of a pet, a plant, an idea, or a business. The Wheel of Life encompasses every phase of life, from the beginning, through growth, to achievement, and reward. It is brilliant in its simplicity.

In the next chapter, you will write complete sentences that describe your planet in a sign in a house. Is your Venus happily operating in personal relationships, in the coveted halls of ivy, or showing a leg behind closed doors? Only your houses will tell you where.

This is when things begin to get way beyond really interesting! You might want to carry on the next chapter's exercises behind closed doors…the information could be tabloid worthy.

BUT HOLD ON FOR A MINUTE! I'm not shouting. That exclamation is written bold and in caps to get your attention. I have a Moon in Sagittarius; I tend to be dramatic.

Please everyone. Read the following section carefully.

Your Window on the World

Mark Twain wrote that the two most important days in your life are the day you were born and the day you find out why.

When you took your first breath on that first important day in your life, the planets stood still in the heavens and, at that moment, determined your astrological chart. Your chart holds the key to possibly understanding the second most important day in your life, the reason why you were born. At the very least, it can point you in the right direction.

One most important key in your chart is your Ascendant, also known as the Rising Sign. You can find the Ascendant, marked ASC, outside the wheel on the left side in The Natural Zodiac illustration shown at the beginning of this book.

You might wonder why this point, which marks the beginning of the 1st house, is called the Ascendant or Rising Sign. There's a reason. Let me explain.

Imagine you get up at midnight. You step outside and find a spot facing east. If you're directionally challenged, that's the general area where the Sun comes up in the morning.

Imagine that you stand there for a day. If you could see the moving zodiacal wheel in the distance beyond Pluto—you will understand this visual better if you read the introduction—in a 24-hour period, you would see all twelve signs ascending or rising over the eastern horizon. When you took your first breath, that wheel stopped for you, marking the exact degree, in a specific sign, as your Ascendant.

So you see, the heavens did stop in honor of your birth! You knew it all along. They stopped to mark the moment you took your first breath; in that moment, you looked at the world through your personal window, your Ascendant. In every chart erected with the correct birth time, this sign on the outside of the wheel at the beginning of the 1st house marks the all important Ascendant.

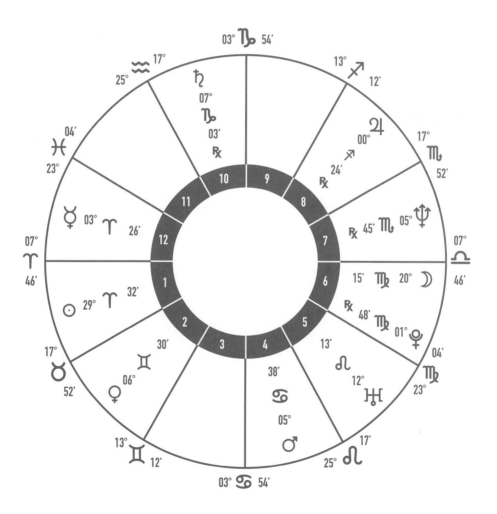

HELEN'S CHART

Our example chart: Helen was born at 4:10 a.m. Her chart is shown here. The sign on the outside of the wheel at the start of the 1st house is Aries. Helen has an Aries Ascendant.

Why is this so important?

Your Ascendant is important because it is your window on the world. The sign that resides on your Ascendant colors the window through which you look every morning when you open your eyes. This sign explains your daily approach to life and your everyday outlook. It also describes your physical body and mannerisms. In a general sense, people see you through this sign. The Ascendant determines so much about your destiny.

In the chart shown here, Helen can't wait to get up and get moving. Full of energy, she races through her morning rituals to prepare to launch into her day. She often bumps into the front door frame on her way out to her sporty car to press the pedal to the metal looking forward to the adventures that await out there.

Look at your chart; find that point at the beginning of your 1st house. The sign on the outside of your wheel is your Ascendant. Turn back to the chapter that describes the signs. Find yours. It will give a thumbnail sketch about how you approach the world every day when you open your eyes. That sign is your window on the world.

Because the turning zodiacal wheel stops at the exact time of day of your birth, it also puts your planets into their proper houses. Now you see why the exact time of day is important.

The comments—I think the time was somewhere around . . . or I'm pretty sure it was . . . or it was close to—won't cut it. The Ascendant is based upon the exact time of day; it sets up the rest of your chart, placing your planets in their correct houses. Without stopping the turning of the wheel at your exact birth time, your planets could be in any one of the twelve houses and your Ascendant could be any one of the twelve signs.

It is worth the time and effort to obtain a copy of your birth certificate to verify the time of your birth. I know mom was there but, believe me, she was pretty busy at the time. In my thirty-plus years of experience in this field, I have heard many strange tales about why the birth time was off, even when mom swore she knew the time. How about the fire engine tearing by the hospital at 10:00 in the morning when mom claims you were born at noon because she heard the church bells ringing.

You are investing your time and effort so, if you want to examine a chart, yours or the chart of someone else, be sure you have the correct time, if at all possible.

IF YOU HAVE A CHART WITHOUT A BIRTH TIME
Again, not shouting. Just getting your attention.

For those of you who don't know your exact time of day, you will have received a noontime chart from me. If you already have a chart without the time, it may be either a noontime or sunrise chart. In either case, your chart shows what signs most of your planets are in, but your chart cannot tell you what houses your planets occupy or what your Ascendant is. Therefore, you won't know what sign defines your window on the world or where in your life the planetary action is playing out.

Do make an effort to find the exact time of day of your birth. Records have been kept in some states for well over a hundred years—and I suspect you're not quite that old. Do check with the town/city hall where you were born. If the time isn't on the copy you receive, ask the clerk if the time is registered on the original copy they have. You can also check with the Bureau of Vital Statistics in the capital of your state. Again, if the time is not noted on the copy you receive, talk to someone at the bureau. Other places where your time of day might be recorded are in county records, baby books, newspaper announcements, and, if this was done during the period you were born, the family Bible.

As a last measure, there are astrologers who specialize in what is called "rectification." They will take the major events in your life and try to match them with specific positions and movements of the planets for the day you were born. It is a timely, and sometimes, expensive process.

It's best to play detective and find your time of day.

How are you doing? Ready to move on? Good.

CHAPTER FIVE

Getting to Know More About Yourself

We're behind closed doors now . . . you're safe from prying eyes, so let it all hang out.

Your chart reveals it all anyway, which you will discover when you begin writing sentences about your planets in their signs in their houses. If you have a chart without the time of day you were born, work with someone else's chart—a child, friend, mate, or someone famous. And keep looking for your birth time. I was adopted and, after a lengthy search, I found my time.

So, let's begin. Line up your three sheets of paper with the Planets on the left, the Signs in the middle, and the Houses on the right. (Now aren't you glad you followed the instructions and wrote them out?)

Using these three sheets as guides, write a sentence about your Ascendant (how you see the world), then take each of the first seven planets in your chart—the Moon, Sun, Mercury, Venus, Mars, Jupiter, and Saturn—and write a simple sentence about each one of them. Finally, address the three outer planets—Uranus, Neptune, and Pluto.

Let's try a few examples:

Examples:

ASC
Your Window on the World

Leo Ascendant:
When I wake up, I look out my window with happiness and a spark of creative energy.

The sentence explained:
When I wake up, I look out my window (ASC) with happiness and a spark of creative energy (Leo).

ASC

Virgo Ascendant:
When I wake up, I look out my window and I'm ready to go to work and get the job done as perfectly as I can.

The sentence explained:
When I wake up, I look out my window (ASC) and I'm ready to go to work and get the job done as perfectly (Virgo) as I can.

The Moon
The Principle: Emotion

Moon in Sagittarius in the 5th house:
I express my emotions exuberantly and optimistically through love for my children and in my creative endeavors.

The sentence explained:
I express my emotions (the Moon) exuberantly and optimistically (Sagittarius) through love for my children and in my creative endeavors (the 5th house).

Another example:

Moon in Capricorn in the 11th house:
I express my emotions seriously and professionally with my friends and I work with groups to help others.

The sentence explained:
I express my emotions (the Moon) seriously and professionally (Capricorn) with my friends, and I work with groups to help others (11th house).

Where and how is your Moon going to sweep up everyone in her arms? Write a sentence about your Moon in its sign in its house.

The Sun
The Principle: Identity

Sun in Scorpio in the 4th house:
I express my identity by intensely protecting my home and privacy.

The same sentence explained:
I express my identity (Sun) by intensely protecting (Scorpio) my home (4th house) and privacy (Scorpio).

Another example:

Sun in Libra in the 7th house:
I express my identity through fair and peaceful one-on-one relationships.

The same sentence explained:
I express my identity (Sun) through fair and peaceful (Libra) one-on-one relationships (7th house).

Where are you going to express your identity, and let your true self shine through? Write a sentence about your Sun in its sign in its house.

Mercury
The Principle: Communication

Mercury in Aquarius in the 6th house:
I communicate and think in an independent and inventive manner at work and about health issues.

The same sentence explained:
I communicate and think (Mercury) in an independent and inventive manner (Aquarius) at work and about health issues (6th house).

Another example:

Mercury in Taurus in the 2nd house:
I communicate and think practically and sensibly about my personal security.

The same sentence explained:
I communicate and think (Mercury) practically and sensibly (Taurus) about my personal security (2nd house).

Where are you discussing issues that are important to you? Where does your mind seem to wander? Write a sentence about your Mercury in its sign in its house.

Venus

The Principle: Attraction

Venus in Cancer in the 9th house:
I attract others by expressing my love emotionally and sympathetically through my philosophy.

The same sentence explained:
I attract others by expressing my love (Venus) emotionally and sympathetically (Cancer) through my philosophy (9th house).

Another example:

Venus in Leo in the 3rd house:
I attract others by expressing my love generously and optimistically in my local community and with siblings and neighbors.

The same sentence explained:
I attract others by expressing my love (Venus) generously and optimistically (Leo) in my local community and with siblings and neighbors (3rd house).

What does your Venus attract? Where does she find love and beauty? Write a sentence about your Venus in its sign in its house.

Mars
The Principle: Action

Mars in Virgo in the 1st house:
I put energy into industriously taking care of my physical body.

The same sentence explained:
I put energy (Mars) into industriously (Virgo) taking care of my physical body (1st house).

Another example:

Mars in Pisces in the 10th house:
I act compassionately in my career.

The same sentence explained:
I act (Mars) compassionately (Pisces) in my career (10th house).

Where do you stir things up? Where is the action? Harness Mars and write a sentence about its sign and house placement.

And now the social planets…

Jupiter
The Principle: Expansion

♃ ♈ 12H

Jupiter in Aries in the 12th house:
I expand and grow positively and ethically by being assertive when working behind the scenes for those less fortunate.

The same sentence explained:
I expand and grow positively and ethically (Jupiter) by being assertive (Aries) when working behind the scenes for those less fortunate (12th house).

Another example.

♃ ♊ 9H

Jupiter in Gemini in the 9th house:
I expand and grow ethically by exploring a multitude of ideas about philosophies and other cultures.

The same sentence explained:
I expand and grow ethically (Jupiter) by exploring a multitude of ideas (Gemini) about philosophies and other cultures (9th house).

Where are you going to grow? Find out where your cosmic help is coming from. Write a sentence describing your Jupiter in its sign in its house.

Saturn
The Principle: Contraction
Focus and Responsibility

Saturn in Cancer in the 4th house:
I take responsibility for protecting my home and family heritage.

The same sentence explained:
I take responsibility (Saturn) for protecting (Cancer) my home and family heritage (4th house).

Another example:

Saturn in Aquarius in the 3rd house:
I focus on being detached but caring and impartial in my everyday communications.

The same sentence explained:
I focus on (Saturn) being detached but caring and impartial (Aquarius) in my everyday communications (3rd house).

Where is the finger-shaker in your chart? Where should you focus? What are your rules? Where is your inner authority? You'll find out by writing a sentence describing your Saturn in its sign in its house.

You see how this works? Great!

Now that you've written sentences about your Ascendant and the first seven planets in their signs in their houses in your chart, we'll discuss the outer planets: Uranus, Neptune, and Pluto.

But, in case you didn't write those sentences, I'll wait. This might take a while, so I'll be back in about twenty minutes. The laundry's done, and now it's going in the dryer. And my kitties, Sashi and Elvis, just knocked over my decorative mason jar that was filled with colored stones. They're so cute!

I'll put on a soft melody so you can relax . . .

I'm back. See how easy it was to write your sentences?

Again, you can analyze the charts of your parents, mate, siblings, children, friends, your cat and dog…yes, they have charts, too. So do businesses and countries. Anything that is "born," anything that has a beginning, has an astrological chart. But for now, let's focus on you.

Now let's look at the three outer planets in your chart—Uranus, Neptune, and Pluto.

As mentioned earlier, because the outer planets move so slowly around the solar system, therefore, around the earth and around you (astrology is an earth-centered view), the three outer planets rule larger segments of the population. In the case of Uranus, it is you and your peers. With Neptune, and Pluto, it is your generation. So take into consideration the signs that your three outer planets are in but, for now, let's concentrate on the house position in which they have taken up residence.

Uranus

The Principle: Awakening
7 years in a sign; 84 years around the chart

In what house in your chart is Uranus, that wild, odd, crazy, and innovative planet? Where are you and your peers acting up? You who are more daring will gladly welcome Uranus into your house to break the rules, and you'll enjoy every minute of it. Those of you who are more conservative still have a rebel lurking in the background somewhere. You may board up the windows and reinforce the doors, but it's too late; Uranus is already in the house.

Some examples:

Uranus in the 7th house:
I like unpredictable, exciting relationships that don't tie me down.

The same sentence explained:
I like unpredictable, exciting (Uranus) relationships (7th house) that don't tie me down (Uranus).

Another example:

Uranus in the 9th house:
I will not be tied down by conventional belief systems or traditional education.

The same sentence explained:
I will not be tied down (Uranus) by conventional belief systems or traditional education (9th house).

Where is your wild and crazy Uranus? Write it down…we all want to know.

I have Uranus in the 10th house of career and public recognition. Some in the public know I'm an astrologer; others who don't know what I do just think I'm odd and different. It works for me; heaven forbid anyone thinks I'm normal! As I read somewhere, the definition of normal is someone "devoid of any outstanding characteristics." Uranus in the 10th house would lead the individual toward an unusual profession.

Neptune
The Principle: Transcendence
14 years in a sign; 164 years around the chart

Neptune transcends boundaries and washes you in a sea of spirituality, creativity, compassion, mysticism, and boundless imagination. Your psychic antenna is tuned in where your Neptune floats. And there's most likely an element of self-sacrifice in the house where you find this planet. Your generation had Neptune in the same sign for 14 years. Look to the house where your Neptune lives.

Examples of Neptune in a house:

Neptune in the 5th house:
I sacrifice for my children to allow them to have fun and develop their talents. Since they were little, I've been able to sense what they like.

The same sentence explained:
I sacrifice (Neptune) for my children to allow them to have fun and develop their creative talents (5th house). Since they were little, I've been able to sense (Neptune) what they like.

Another example:

Neptune in the 11th house:
I work with the group, sacrificing my time to support my chosen charity. And I often sense who will be the biggest contributors.

The same sentence explained:
I work with the group (11th house) sacrificing my time (Neptune) to support my chosen charity (11th house). And I often sense (Neptune) who will be the biggest contributors.

Where does your compassion lead you? Where are you willing to sacrifice? Write a sentence about the house in which your Neptune boat floats.

Pluto

The Principle: Transformation
12-31 years in a sign; 248 years around the chart

And then there's powerful Pluto. Pluto is way, way back behind closed doors, dressed in black, in control, hidden from everyday scrutiny. This planet is the power behind the throne. In what house does your power reside, and where do you need to control and transform your life? Your generation had Pluto in the same sign for anywhere between 12 and 31 years, depending upon the sign. Pluto doesn't linger long in Scorpio—it's too intense.

Examples of Pluto in a house:

Pluto in the 3rd house:
I transform how I think and communicate so that the power of my thoughts and words will totally change my life and the lives of those with whom I communicate.

The same sentence explained:
I transform (Pluto) how I think and communicate (3rd house) so that the power of my thoughts and words (3rd house) will totally change (Pluto) my life and the lives of those with whom I communicate.

Another example:

Pluto in the 4th house:
I transform my home and my roots so that my family will be born into a better existence.

The same sentence explained:
I transform (Pluto) my home and my roots (4th house) so that my family will be born (Pluto) into a better existence.

Where is your Pluto hiding? Bring it into the light of awareness by writing a sentence describing the house in which it is lurking.

CHAPTER SIX

Your Sentencing

Ready for your sentencing?

That didn't come out quite right. Let me try again.

It's time to make what I call a "Sentencing Sheet." It is at this point you find out why you wrote three separate sheets labeled Planets, Signs, and Houses, along with their key words. Please tell me you did because, if you did, you can now make your own Sentencing Sheet using the key words you wrote. If you didn't . . . well, back to the drawing board.

The Sentencing Sheet is a great tool to have on hand while you're learning astrology. It contains key words for the planets, the signs, and the houses, and will aid you in composing simple but accurate sentences for each planet's position in an astrological chart.

Please see the Sentencing Sheet I have composed. I coined a few new adverbs, which you will find listed under "How it is expressed." If Merriam-Webster can add new words like "hashtag" and "selfie" to the dictionary, as was done in 2014, I figure I can stick in a few awkward ones here for your benefit.

The sentences may sound awkward, but they are accurate. Try reading a few just to get the sense of how to use the Sentencing Sheet.

You might say:

My love (Venus) is expressed harmoniously (Libra) through my daily communication and language (House 3).

Or: My drive (Mars) is expressed seriously (Capricorn) through my work and in taking care of my health (House 6).

Or: My focus and responsibility (Saturn) is expressed intensely (Scorpio) where I work selflessly for others (House 12).

SENTENCING SHEET

The Principle	How it is expressed	Where it is expressed
Sun Identity | Ego Individuation	Aries Assertively | Competitively Courageously | Self-centeredly	House 1: Personal Outlook | Health Physical Body | New Beginnings
Moon Emotion | Instinct Nurture	Taurus Patiently | Stably Sensually | Possessively Stubbornly	House 2: Values | Self-Worth Personal Money | Possessions Talents | Five Senses
Mercury Communication Reasoning Decision Making	Gemini Intellectually | Cleverly Quickly | Scatteredly	House 3: Communication Learning Language | Local Community | Siblings
Venus Love and Beauty Values | Self-Worth	Cancer Cautiously | Emotionally Tenaciously | Protectively Psychically	House 4: Home | Family | Parents Heritage | Land | Conservation | Parent in the Home
Mars Action | Energy Drive	Leo Generously | Creatively Proudly | Boastfully	House 5: Personal Creativity Love | Children | Games | Sports Fun | Gambling
Jupiter Growth Expansion | Ethics	Virgo Industriously | Modestly Analytically | Critically	House 6: Work and Health | Diet Food | Small Pets | Social Services | Police/Military
Saturn Focus | Responsibility Discipline	Libra Peacefully | Artistically Harmoniously | Indecisively	House 7: One-on-One Relationships | Contracts | Arbitration
Uranus (Read House Position Only) Freedom Rebellion Originality Awakening	Scorpio Intensely | Probingly Privately | Suspiciously Psychically Sagittarius Enthusiastically Directly | Philosophically Exaggeratingly	House 8: Joint Monies | Taxes Wills | Sex | Birth/Death/Change Mysteries | Magic | Research House 9: Philosophy | Religion Higher Education | Teaching | Foreign Countries | Long Trips | The Law and Courts
Neptune (Read House Position Only) Compassion Imagination Spirituality	Capricorn Seriously | Cautiously Ambitiously | Coldly Aquarius Independently | Tolerantly Impersonally | Rebelliously Intuitively	House 10: Career | Public Reputation | Honors | Fame | Success Employer | Authority Figures | Parent Outside the Home House 11: Friends | Groups Clubs | Organizations | Hopes | Wishes | Ideals | Humanitarian Work Charities
Pluto (Read House Position Only) Transformation Resurrection	Pisces Compassionately Humorously | Timidly Sacrificially | Psychically	House 12: Wisdom | Inspiration Artistry | Charity Work Behind the Scenes | Seclusion: Retreats | Hospitals | Prisons

Take the time to make one for yourself with the key words for the planets, the signs, and the houses that speak to you. Be creative and imaginative. Realize that what you write isn't written in stone; you can change or add more words as you progress in your studies.

With this sheet, you can compose simple sentences to describe your planetary placements as well as those of your family, friends, and don't forget the pets.

For classes, I put a sentencing sheet on a piece of card stock as an example for my students. The card stock is sturdier. Some students have laminated their own Sentencing Sheets and use them as references in classes and at home as they learn on their own.

The previous chapters on the planets, signs, and houses were constructed so that you could get a quick peek at how astrology works. It was done in this manner so you wouldn't become overwhelmed and then discouraged with too much information while you are just beginning to learn this subject.

Coming up, we have more ground to cover. You do need a strong foundation upon which to build the future chapters so, it's worth the time and patience to get the first five chapters in this book under your belt. Feel them in your gut, and then make sure they're tucked securely into the wrinkled crevices of your mind so that you understand them intellectually.

You could keep your Sentencing Sheet and The Natural Zodiac illustration handy while you go back and review. Now that you know a bit more about the information contained on those two pieces, they will help reinforce what you have already learned.

If you need to, go back and review the previous chapters. You've got plenty of time; there's no need to rush. This is a lifetime investment. You'll be glad you did.

When you're ready, let's find out who rules the astrological signs in the natural zodiac. Someone has to be in charge, right? Since Scorpio rules my 4th house of the home, you know who's in charge here. But I digress.

CHAPTER SEVEN

More About the Signs

Okay . . . close your eyes and take a deep breath. Roll your shoulders . . . ready?

As I just mentioned, somebody has to be in charge of the signs, right? We can't have them floating out there without planetary direction. They're not rudderless because each sign has an affinity with a planet, or planets, so let's talk about that.

Before the discovery of Uranus in 1781, there were seven original planets, and they were associated with specific signs. The farthest planet from the Earth that could be seen with the naked eye was Saturn; it was called the ring-pass-not. The world up to that point operated under the dictates of structured Saturn. To a great extent, you obeyed the traditional rules, followed in your parents' footsteps, and respected the mores of the time. Of course, there were always exceptions but, in general, life was pretty much determined by the society into which you were born.

Prior to 1781, astrologers knew of the seven planets only—the Moon, the Sun, Mercury, Venus, Mars, Jupiter, and Saturn. Therefore, they assigned each of these seven planets to specific signs with which they had affinities.

PLANETARY RULERS

In the illustration above, notice that the Moon who rules Cancer is in the 4th house, and the Sun who rules Leo is in the 5th house.

Starting at the 4th and 5th houses, and using the planets Mercury, Venus, Mars, Jupiter, and Saturn, in that order, work your way around the wheel in both directions, clockwise and counterclockwise. You will find that Mercury rules both Gemini and Virgo; Venus rules both Taurus and Libra; Mars rules both Aries and Scorpio; Jupiter rules both Pisces and Sagittarius; and Saturn rules both Aquarius and Capricorn.

These were and still are the rulers of those signs.

Nice and neat. I do like that symmetry. Too bad Uranus had to come along in 1781 and break things up.

But of course, that's its job. It breaks the mold of tradition to allow us more freedom to explore and create and express our individuality. It releases the pressures that build up and hold us back. I did mention earlier that Uranus rules earthquakes and volcanic eruptions, releasing hidden pressure from beneath the earth. It also rules lightning and electricity, those elements that shock.

Well, when Uranus was discovered, it did indeed shock the world, releasing it from the dictates of the negative aspects of Saturnian society. Remember the American Revolution, Franklin and his kite experiments in an attempt to learn more about the nature of lightning and electricity, and the Industrial Revolution? And, of course, there was the French Revolution that overthrew the long established monarchy. "Let them eat cake," did not go over well.
The world was about to change dramatically. Individuals found they didn't have to always follow the rules; they were willing to rebel.

Astrologers welcomed this new planet with open arms. With the discovery of Uranus in 1781, they eventually found that this newly viewed planet was most compatible with the sign Aquarius, the sign that promotes the free expression of the independent and inventive individual who demands a voice in the world. So Aquarius now had two ruling planets: Saturn and Uranus.

In 1846, with the discovery of mystical Neptune, the watery planet that brought in psychoanalysis, spiritualism, the camera and films, astrologers realized that this planet could only rule the sign Pisces, the sign that transcends barriers, and is in contact with worlds beyond the physical. Remember, the Ouija Board came along shortly after this discovery. So, Pisces then had two rulers: Jupiter and Neptune.

And finally, in 1930, with the discovery of Pluto, the planet that coincided with the emergence of atomic weaponry and the potential for mass destruction, the rise of the underworld, and the pronouncement of The Big Bang Theory, astrologers knew that this planet could only rule Scorpio, the sign of birth, death, and transformation. So, today Scorpio is ruled by Mars and Pluto.

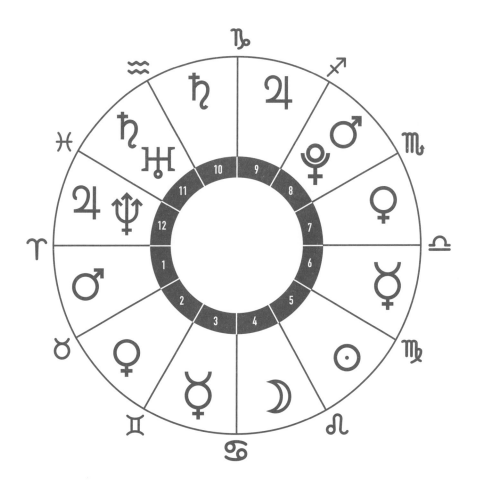

EXTRA PLANETARY RULERS

See the illustration above with the three outer planets added.

Now, look at your sheet titled Signs—the one you constructed back in chapter 2— where you listed the signs with their symbols and key words. Add the appropriate planetary rulers to their signs. Notice how the energies of the planets complement the behavior of the signs to which they are assigned.

You might want to spend some time with these planetary rulers, and let the correlations sink in.

For now, we will go through a brief examination of how these planets fit into the signs they rule, starting with the Moon and the Sun, and working around the wheel in both directions.

It will be helpful if you refer to the illustration and the Natural Zodiac as you read the following descriptions.

The Moon is happy nestled in the sign Cancer where it ferociously protects its own.

The Sun is brilliantly at home in Leo where it shines happiness, exploring and expressing love through its own creative energy—through children, love affairs, and artistic and entertaining enterprises—and where it inspires the creativity of the young and the young at heart.

Mercury in Gemini is happy flitting from one flowering energy station to another, tasting a variety of flavors, in pursuit of multiple experiences.

Mercury in Virgo is tasked with taking that information and putting it into useful organized form.

Venus in Taurus loves to embrace all that it owns…my body, my food, my money, my resources…because it is a matter of personal survival.

Venus in Libra loves beauty, art, and relationships where it is able to communicate, share, and enjoy interacting with others one-on-one.

Mars works dynamically in Aries, bolting forward headfirst, unstoppable, in the pursuit of adventure.

Mars in Scorpio is just as dynamic, only now it is fixed and contained, putting its considerable energy into protecting the life it has created and ensuring that those commodities necessary for that life to continue are protected.

Pluto in Scorpio knows that the issues of birth, life, death, and resources need to be heavily monitored; this planet is the hidden protector, intense and controlling.

Jupiter in Sagittarius is happy expanding knowledge accumulated from the cultures of the world through communication, long trips, higher education, and teaching.

Jupiter in Pisces covers that boundless watery realm where the accumulated knowledge now translates into wisdom.

Neptune in Pisces transcends the boundary between the physical world and the world of spirit, where all the efforts of the material world no longer matter; where the yearning for connection with something greater than itself is all that matters.

Saturn is totally focused in Capricorn because it is responsible for the structures that house the accumulated laws that hold society together, and it also rules the people who are in charge of those structures. Saturn in Capricorn keeps the world contained and orderly.

You might ask what Saturn is doing as a ruler of independent free-thinking Aquarius. That is a very good question.

Prior to the discovery of Uranus in 1781, the big wide world was ruled by Saturn, the ring-pass-not. Everyone had to follow the rules; there was no room for free thinkers or individual freedom. Aquarians had a most difficult time before the discovery of Uranus, like experiencing house arrest, dunking in the nearest pond, burning at the stake, and other practices too horrifying to think about. Back in those days, when Aquarians were confronted with "new" concepts and ideas, they had to keep their discoveries under Saturnian wraps, working within the confines of accepted ideas. Many of the great ones managed to survive, as noted by ancient and medieval inventions and writings.

Today, there are scientists who seem determined to stay with the tried and true. A case in point: When French statistician Michel Gauquelin set out to disprove astrology by statistically analyzing thousands of professional peoples' birth charts (from 1959–1965) to determine if the planet ruling their profession was highlighted in their charts, he found it was statistically true. It changed his mind about astrological influences. When presenting his statistics to fellow scientists, French Academy member Jean Rostand remarked, "If statistics are used to prove astrology, then I no longer believe in statistics." This is a Saturnian scientist, rather than an Aquarian scientist. (*Larousse Encyclopedia of Astrology,* New American Library, 1977, p.118)

Uranus that wild and crazy rascal also rules the wild and crazy sign, Aquarius, along with Saturn. Now the skies are the limit for Aquarians, experienced today by this new Aquarian Age and the worldwide communications revolution.

You might want to go back and reread the section on the twelve signs to get the full impact of these rulerships. They will be important if and when you decide to continue your studies at another time.

For now, please study what we have discussed to this point so that it is second nature to you. Again, this course was taught over many months to allow students the time to absorb the information in stages.

At this point, be sure that you...

- Know the planets in order and the principles they represent
- Know the signs in order and what energies they define
- Know the rulers of those signs and how they have an affinity with their signs
- Know the meanings of the houses

Pull out your copy of the Natural Zodiac—yes, you can look at it again. Study it. You will find that it is beginning to make sense to you.

If you are at that place where you can comfortably discuss the above points, then it's time to trip the light fantastic and learn even more about the signs.

I know you're wondering where that expression came from. "Trip" in this sense means to dance in an imaginative manner. You can thank the seventeenth century poet John Milton for that clever segue.

CHAPTER EIGHT

Your Trips and Quads

As we left the last chapter, we were talking about tripping the light fantastic, but we can't leave out the Quads.

Trips and Quads are working partners.

This combo is beginning to sound more like an exercise program in a muscle-bound gym, I know. But believe me, the only muscles you have to exercise here are those little gray cells. They say every time you learn something new, another wrinkle appears in your brain.

This does remind me of an old television commercial for prunes where an elderly, dignified English actor proclaimed that the problem with prunes was that they were "rather badly wrinkled . . ." A rather badly wrinkled brain is a compliment!

Where was I? Oh, yes. The signs are divided into two groups called the Quadruplicities and the Triplicities.

Big words but they simply mean a grouping of the astrological signs in fours, the Quadruplicites, and a grouping of the astrological signs in threes, the Triplicities.

By counting the number of planets plus your Ascendant that reside in each of these two categories, you can determine two things: how your "action meter" registers and what kind of temperament you have.

The Quadruplicities reveal your action meter, or how you take action. Are you up and on your feet at dawn's early light, ready to rumble, or does it take a crane to get you out of bed in the morning? Then again, maybe you're restless, up most of the night, pacing the floor, raiding the refrigerator, and blaming it on the full moon, even when it's not full.

The Triplicities reveal your temperament. Are you calm and steady, or fiery and energetic? Or perhaps more intellectually and socially inclined. Or are you reaching for the box of tissues during reruns of *Lassie*? The Triplicities are your answer.

We will start with the Quadruplicities; it's time to flex your muscles so let's examine how you start your engines.

The Quadruplicities

We divide the 12 signs into three groups, which are called Cardinal, Fixed, and Mutable. These three groups define your action meter. They show how you take action, your method of operating (M/O).

Cardinal signs initiate the action; they take the lead and move out. Their action meter needle is in the red danger zone.

Fixed signs don't like to move; they're set and don't like change. Their action meter needle does not move, even during earthquakes and hurricanes.

Mutable signs are flexible; they change easily. Their action meter needle sways back and forth, like a weeping willow in the wind.

Forgive my hyperbole. I do think that visual images register more than words. And I do want you to remember these three categories.

These three modes of action show how you start your engine. It also reflects somewhat on your behavior. Are you naughty or nice? We're about to find out. But don't worry; it's our secret.

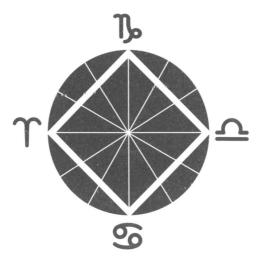

The Cardinal Signs are Aries, Cancer, Libra, and Capricorn. Cardinal signs are those who initiate activity; they're always in forward motion.

See the illustration that follows. Notice that the lines connecting the signs in the Cardinal Quadruplicity form a square. These signs register high on the action meter; actively exuding energy and initiating activity.

Initiating Aries takes off to explore new horizons with boundless energy, never looking back.

Initiating Cancer is driven to action to protect the young. At first glance, this behavior is not noticeable, but threaten its brood, then watch the ferocious female rise to fight to the death.

Initiating Libra actively seeks out people and relationships with the friendly hand shake, the charming smile, and the how are you and the family and the dogs and the cats and the pet parakeet. And don't you have a pet turtle?

Finally, initiating Capricorn actively pursues its career goals in its sure-footed climb to the top. It's relentless and enduring.

The Cardinal Signs are always at the starting gate, alert, and ready to go at their unique speed and for their specific reasons.

Example:
My grandson has a statistical degree. At the age of four, he was counting the number of measles spots on his brother's chest. (He is very smart. I know—we all think our kids and grandkids are special—and that's the way it should be.) With his intelligence, it might be surprising to find he has a preponderance of active Cardinal Signs; however, today he is actively engaged in outdoor activities. He has done the Tough Mudder, a grueling sports event to raise money for wounded veterans, three times. He runs four or five times a week, although he keeps count of his miles and tallies them at the end of the year. Statistics again. He reminds me of the *Sesame Street* character, the Count.

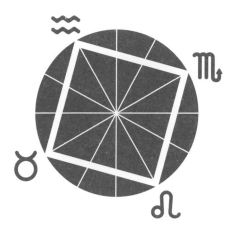

The Fixed Signs are Taurus, Leo, Scorpio, and Aquarius. Fixed signs are fixed, stable, steady, reliable, determined, and anchored. Did I mention they don't move much?

Fixed Taurus stubbornly hangs on to what it has and will never let go—I mean never! It's a matter of personal survival.

Fixed Leo is forever the child on the playground, joyfully immersed in the game of life and in its own creative pleasures. For Leo, it's always recess time; let the games begin, and Leo is always center ring.

Fixed Scorpio intensely guards the resources that will ensure the continuance of life. It truly is a matter of life and death for those in its care.

And fixed Aquarius protects the independent and intellectual freedom of the individual and of humanity as a whole.

The Fixed Signs provide the anchors in life.

Example:
Reid has four planets in Taurus, including his Moon, in the 8th house. He determinedly guards joint resources; his career revolves around finances. He says he must earn money to support his family. I complimented him on his devotion to the financial protection of his family, and suggested that even if he were single, he would feel the same way.

You will remember that in the introduction I spoke about the serpent signs. Taurus, Leo, Scorpio, and Aquarius are the serpent signs. Please refer to the introduction if you need a refresher.

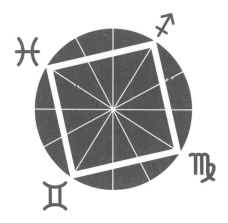

The Mutable Signs are Gemini, Virgo, Sagittarius, and Pisces. The Mutable signs are versatile, adaptable, and flexible.

Flexible Gemini gathers information from all and various sources, never lingering long enough to investigate deeply because it's on to new experiences.

Flexible Virgo takes the information that Gemini has gathered and organizes it into a system that is usable but open to reorganization as new information arrives.

Flexible Sagittarius trumpets accumulated information from the mountaintops, inspiring others with the current knowledge to date. Sagittarius realizes that knowledge continually expands and changes.

And flexible Pisces, wise and full of faith in the next cycle of life, flows on the spiritual currents of universal compassion, knowing that each drop in the ocean changes the sea.

The Mutable Signs are there to remind us that change is constant and necessary for the continuation of life.

Example:
Susan has five mutable signs with a strong emphasis in the 9th. A lawyer, she plans to start her own firm. She has moved away from her strict religious upbringing and has found her voice. She wants to share her earnings with various charitable organizations. She plans to work with firms from her past to introduce spirituality and ethics into their practices.

Granted, if you get a chart from an astrological program, this information may already be on that chart. However, it's important to understand how that information was determined and what it means.

So, let's examine the Quadruplicities in the chart of Helen to determine her action meter, how she gets up and goes. (See her chart on the opposite page.)

In the diagram below, you will find Helen's planets placed in their proper categories of Cardinal, Fixed, and Mutable.

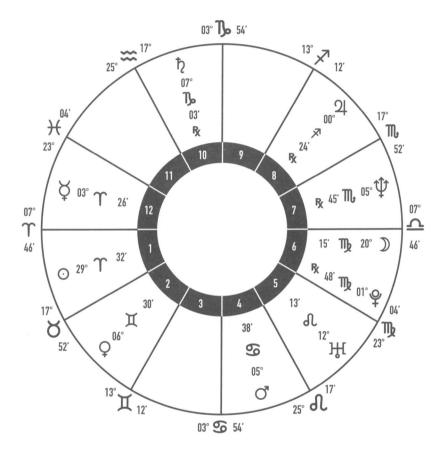

HELEN'S CHART

The Cardinal Signs are Aries, Cancer, Libra, and Capricorn:

In Aries, Helen has her Ascendant, Mercury, and the Sun; in Cancer, she has Mars; in Libra, she has no planets; and in Capricorn, she has Saturn.

The symbols for the Ascendant, Mercury, the Sun, Mars, and Saturn are in the line next to the word Cardinal in the diagram that follows. The total is in the last column.

The Fixed Signs are Taurus, Leo, Scorpio, and Aquarius:

In Taurus, Helen has no planets; in Leo, she has Uranus; in Scorpio, she has Neptune; and in Aquarius, she has no planets.

The symbols for Uranus and Neptune are in the line next to the word Fixed in the diagram below. The total is in the last column.

The Mutable Signs are Gemini, Virgo, Sagittarius, and Pisces:

In Gemini, Helen has Venus; in Virgo, she has Pluto and the Moon; in Sagittarius, she has Jupiter; and in Pisces, she has no planets.

The symbols for Venus, Pluto, the Moon, and Jupiter are in the line next to the word Mutable in the diagram below. The total is in the last column.

Now, add the column on the right. The total is 11: the Ascendant plus the 10 planets.

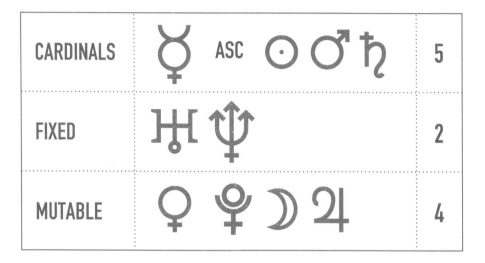

Helen has more emphasis in Cardinal signs with a total of 5. Therefore, she has boundless energy and is always ready to go.

Let's look at your chart.

Follow the same directions we used to determine the Quadruplicites in Helen's chart. Determine the distribution of your planets, and fill in the diagram below. Write the symbols for your planets and your Ascendant on the appropriate lines, and total them in the last column.

CARDINALS	
FIXED	
MUTABLE	

Add the column on the right. The total is 11: your Ascendant plus your 10 planets.

If your planets and Ascendant are more or less evenly distributed amongst Cardinal, Fixed, and Mutable signs, then the way you handle things, your M/O, is well balanced between taking charge, remaining steady, and yet being flexible when the situation requires.

If one group is stronger than the others, then your behavior will exhibit those particular qualities.

And that, my friends, is the Quadruplicities.

Let's discuss how the Quadruplicities carry on. Just so you don't have to flip back to the other pages, the Quadruplicities are pictured here again.

CARDINAL

The Cardinal Signs—Aries, Cancer, Libra, and Capricorn—belong to the same group and are always ready for action but they start their engines in very different ways which, as you will see later, tend to irritate one another.

Aries steps on the gas before you get your leg in the car door.

Cancer sits in the idling car, watching and waiting, in case there's a family emergency, then it's pedal to the metal while the finger dials 911 on the cell phone.

Libra helps his partner step into the car and be comfortably seated. He clips on her seat belt, then seats himself and adjusts the air flow to her liking . . . before turning on the ignition.

Capricorn directs his chauffeur to drive cautiously but expects a police escort to clear the way and get him to the important meeting on time.

I probably don't have to point out how these different driving techniques will cause friction on the road. There'll be honking and cussing and impatience. When planets in one of these signs try to talk to planets in another of these signs, there will be differences of opinion . . . believe it!

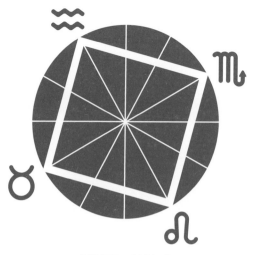

FIXED SIGNS

The Fixed Signs are: Taurus, Leo, Scorpio, and Aquarius. They don't plan to even discuss their burrowed positions, so letting anyone else take charge is verboten.

Taurus won't budge because she already has everything she needs within reach. She feels quite comfortable knowing that all she owns is secured by a 9' razor wire enclosure around her belongings.

Leo won't budge because he is the King, and everyone should come to him, to bask in his glorious radiance. He runs the kingdom, after all. You can't seriously think he would come to you. Who could possibly pass up the opportunity to kneel before him and bask in his generous and royal light?

Scorpio is not budging; no way! She's fortified securely behind the castle walls which are protected by a crocodile infested moat. There are people inside its walls whom she is dedicated to defend and support.

Aquarius won't budge on his beliefs and ideas. He is dedicated to freedom of thought and lifestyle. It's those wacky tats, the purple hair, and the cascades of nose rings that make a statement about the freedom to make choices, to be different in the eyes of the world.

These determined signs express their fixity in very different ways. These are the ones that have the most difficulty in getting along with each other because…well… because they are so fixed…or determined…or shall we say, stubborn as hell. Planets in one fixed sign have a fight on their hands with planets in another fixed sign. But…they will feel sooo good when it's over and resolved. Feel those muscles!

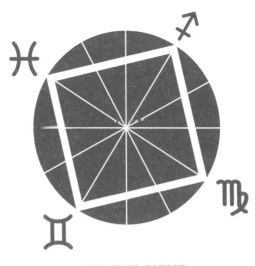

MUTABLE SIGNS

The Mutable Signs—Gemini, Virgo, Sagittarius, and Pisces—are flexible.

Gemini doesn't stay in one place long enough to get stuck on anything.

Virgo's mind is in a constant state of flux. With great efficiency, she flexibly handles all the little bitty pieces…fitting this one into that one, and if that doesn't work, trying another piece…until she manages to put the entire puzzle together. The sweat from her worried brow does leave a damp trail—did she do the job perfectly? What can she change to make it even more perfect?

Sagittarius gathers all the knowledge he can and then pontificates from the rooftops. He does need to heed the warning that the problem is…"some think intelligence is the expansion of knowledge rather than the depth of understanding" (as was quoted in the front of this book). As new information comes along, he eventually adjusts his message.

Pisces is just plain flexible, knowing it will all come out in the wash. She leaves it in the hands of fate. She can swim this way, or she can swim that way. She flows on the tides of life, preparing for the spiritual awakening.

The Mutable Signs, of course, do not understand each other.

Planets in one flexible sign don't understand the methods of planets in one of the other flexible signs, but they can work out their differences with a bit more ease, for the very reason that they are flexible.

Spend time thinking about the Quadruplicites…Cardinal, Fixed, and Mutable. A thorough understanding of them will enhance your ability to understand yourself and others, and to gain a greater understanding of astrology.

You will learn more about how to use the Quadruplicities in the next chapter.

The Triplicities

Now to trip the light fantastic, we take a peek at the **Triplicities**, which determine your temperament, your disposition, and how it affects your behavior.

In the Triplicities, we divide the signs into four groups called Fire, Earth, Air, and Water. Fire is impulsive; earth is materialistic; air is intellectual; and water is emotional, psychic, and spiritual.

We have common expressions that describe these different temperaments: a hot head (Fire), stubborn as a bull (Earth), an air head (Air), a bleeding heart (Water). These less than flattering terms define the underlying meaning of each group.

The three signs that belong to the Fire group, for instance, share the same type of temperament. The same is true for the Earth signs, the Air signs, and the Water signs.

See the illustrations that follow.

Notice that the line connecting the signs in each of the groups—Fire, Earth, Air, and Water—forms a triangle.

Let's examine each group.

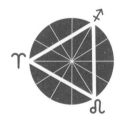

Fire Signs:
The fire signs are Aries, Leo, and Sagittarius.

These three signs have the same dynamic, fiery, outgoing, energetic, and optimistic temperaments, so they understand and get along with each other.

There is the pioneering fire of Aries who leads the pack.

There is the loving, creative fire of Leo that draws you in to be warmed by its flame.

There is the enthusiastic fire of ideas in Sagittarius that stimulate your higher mind.

When you have an abundance of planets in fire signs, you inspire, energize, and lead those around you.

Of course, you can get carried away, like Armando, who has six planets in fire signs. He rides his motorcycle no hands, backwards, kneeling, and sometimes standing up. He just can't seem to get enough of that adrenaline rush.

Earth Signs:
The earth signs are Taurus, Virgo, and Capricorn.

These signs have the same practical, down-to-earth, business-like, hard-working, ambitious temperaments so they understand and get along with each other.

There is the steady, value-conscious, security oriented Taurus.

There is the modest, precise, devoted, hard-working Virgo.

And there is the serious, ambitious, climb the ladder of success to the top of the company Capricorn.

If you have an abundance of planets in these signs, you are dependable and thorough and cautious, focusing on security, work, and career.

Katherine has four planets in Capricorn in her second house of earning money. Extremely organized and focused, she works day and night to secure her future and to make her mark in the world. She doesn't worry about relationships. She said, "Men are a dime a dozen." Even her use of a common expression involves money.

....

Air Signs:
The air signs are Gemini, Libra, and Aquarius.

These signs have the same intellectual and communicative temperaments, so they understand and get along with each other.

There is the curiosity and restlessness of Gemini that collects and disseminates information to all those it encounters.

There is the natural social ability of Libra reaching out to the other side to communicate fairly and to share.

And there is the intuitive understanding and humanitarian impulse of Aquarius that believes in universal laws that protect the intellectual freedom of all people, regardless of background, race, religious beliefs, or sexual orientation.

Melanie has a "gazillion" planets in Libra. She wants to discuss thoughts and ideas until forever. I mean, reaching a conclusion would take the fun out of the debate. Her husband has been known to roll off the couch, glassy eyed, with a hand clutched to his chest in order to get her to change the subject…and to get her laughing. It usually works.

Water Signs:
The water signs are Cancer, Scorpio, and Pisces.

These signs have the same emotional, psychic, and spiritual temperaments so they understand and get along with each other.

There is the emotionally, fiercely protective Cancer who is wrapped up in family and remembering the past, and who is extremely protective of new life in the home/family/business.

There is the emotionally intense Scorpio who instinctively understands how to find the resources necessary to protect those in its care so that life will prevail.

And there is the emotionally spiritual Pisces whose psychic bathing in the sea of spirituality reaffirms faith in the cycles of life.

Years ago, I talked with a young man in his late twenties who had four Pisces planets crowding his Ascendant. Surrounded by an almost ethereal energy field, his liquid eyes seemed depthless. I asked if he yearned for something beyond the physical world. He said that he had spent most of his twenties in a monastery.

So there you have the Triplicities—Fire, Earth, Air, and Water—which are indicators of the four different temperaments. Fire, Earth, Air, and Water are also called the Elements

....

Let's examine Helen's chart once again (see page 116), this time for the Triplicities.

In the diagram that follows, Helen's planets are placed in their proper categories.

First, look at the fire signs: Aries, Leo, and Sagittarius:

In Aries, Helen has her Ascendant, her Mercury, and her Sun; in Leo, she has Uranus; and in Sagittarius, she has Jupiter.

The symbols for the Ascendant, Mercury, the Sun, Uranus, and Jupiter are written in the line next to the word Fire in the diagram below. The total is in the last column.

The earth signs are Taurus, Virgo, and Capricorn:

In Taurus, Helen has no planets; in Virgo, she has Pluto and the Moon; and in Capricorn, she has Saturn.

The symbols for Pluto, the Moon, and Saturn are written in the line next to the word Earth in the diagram that follows. The total is in the last column.

The air signs are Gemini, Libra, and Aquarius:

In Gemini, Helen has Venus; in Libra, she has no planets; in Aquarius, she has no planets.

The symbol for Venus is next to the word Air in the diagram below. The total is in the last column.

The water signs are Cancer, Scorpio, and Pisces:

In Cancer, Helen has Mars; in Scorpio, she has Neptune; and in Pisces, she has no planets.

The symbols for Mars and Neptune are written on the line next to the word Water in the diagram below. The total is in the last column.

Now, add the column on the right. The total is 11; her Ascendant and her 10 planets.

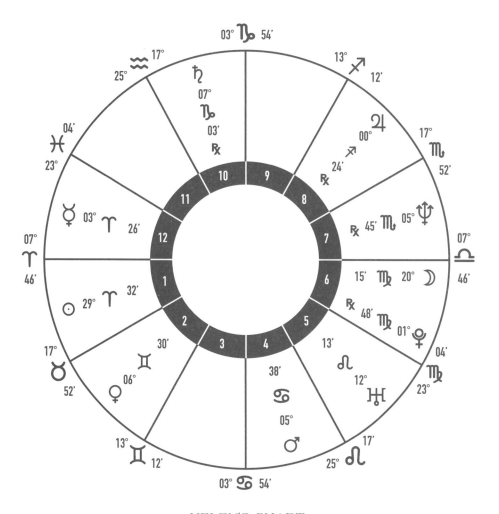

HELEN'S CHART

You have just determined that Helen has 5 Fire signs, therefore, her personality is fiery and energetic.

FIRE	☿ ASC ☉ ♅ ♃	5
EARTH	♀♇ ☽ ♄	3
AIR	♀	1
WATER	♂ ♆	2

Look for the Triplicities in your chart. Fill in the diagram below, writing the symbols for your planets and your Ascendant on the appropriate lines, and total them in the last column.

The total will be 11: your Ascendant and your 10 planets.

FIRE		
EARTH		
AIR		
WATER		

If your planets are evenly distributed amongst the four elements of Fire, Earth, Air, and Water, your temperament is evenly balanced. If there is preponderance in Fire signs, you are more impulsive, adventurous, and quick to act; if in Earth signs, you are stable, patient, security conscious, and believe that slow-and-steady wins the race; if in Air signs, you are more social, intellectual and non-discriminating; and if in water signs, you are more emotional, psychic, and spiritual.

You will learn more about the Triplicities of Fire, Earth, Air, and Water, in the next chapter when we discuss aspects.

Your Signature

Once you have determined your Quadruplicities and Triplicities, you have what's called the signature of your chart.

In Helen's chart, we determined from the Quadruplicities that her action meter is Cardinal. We determined through the Triplicities that her temperament is Fire.

Therefore, Helen's signature is Cardinal Fire (CF), which is the most active and dynamic of all the signatures. This explains her extremely active, energetic, on-the-move lifestyle.

What is your signature?

You may find that your Quadruplicities and Triplicities are as evenly balanced as possible. In that case, you don't have a specific signature; you operate smoothly in both categories.

If you do have a specific signature, look at the illustration of The Natural Zodiac (page 9). Inside one of the inner rings, you will find there are double capital letters for each sign of the zodiac.

Notice that Aries is labeled CF, which means Cardinal Fire, the most active of all the signs of the zodiac. Your signature might be Fixed Earth (FE), which is Taurus; or Mutable Water (MW), which is Pisces; or Cardinal Air (CA), which is Libra. You see how that works.

When you know who you are, and you know with whom you are interacting, you have the keys to good relationships. To tell someone like Helen who is active, and always on the go, to settle down, stay at home, hand the car keys over to her mate, and be a happy homemaker, is fruitless and just plain wrong. She is doing what she should be doing.

We must refrain from giving advice to others from the center of our own wheel. Unless we can stand in the center of that person's wheel with them and try to see the world through their eyes, the best we can do is understand from "whence they come." And hope they do the same for us.

A final note here: sometimes, if an individual has no planets in one of the cardinal, fixed, or mutable signs, or if they have no planets in Fire, Earth, Air, or Water signs, she may be drawn to that missing piece. She may work harder at that missing piece because of a subconscious desire to make up for what seems to be lacking in her life.

For instance, I have one Air sign yet . . . from the time I was five years old, I wanted to be a writer. I asked so many questions growing up that the adults in my home threatened to paint a question mark on my forehead to warn others as I approached. To this date, I have written eight books, two newspaper columns, and numerous magazine articles. My profession is astrology, which I have taught, and I consult with clients every week. You might say I have overcompensated for my one Air sign.

Whew! That was a lot to absorb.

So, for now, take a few days to go over the prior information. This chapter contains important information that will help you understand astrology so much better. Don't rush. Remember, astrology is a structure that requires one building block at a time. The foundation has to be stable and sturdy before you can set more upon it.

I'll wait while you go back and reread this chapter once, maybe twice…who knows, perhaps even three times. Three times the charm, as they say. Whoever "they" are.

I'm waiting…take your time…

All set? Okay.

In Chapter 10, we will put it all together. Following that, in chapter 11, we're going to peek through your astrological window and eavesdrop on the planets. Doesn't matter if the shades are drawn. Astrology, like the Shaolin priest, walks through walls.

CHAPTER NINE

Putting It All Together

Way back on page 9, I declared, "Don't look at the next page . . . You do remember that, don't you? The warm chocolate chip cookies cooling on the kitchen counter, and all that? And how I promised that the information on the illustration would eventually make sense to you?

I'm sure you do remember…that is, unless you skipped all the preliminaries and started on chapter 1.

If you did start this book with chapter 1, you will remember that I said I read a book from cover to cover. That way I don't miss anything.

Just in case you missed that early page before Chapter 1, the same illustration titled The Natural Zodiac is reprinted on page 122. This is where we put it all together.

Let's look at that wheel. Note that the designations are counterclockwise because of the direction of the Earth's rotation.

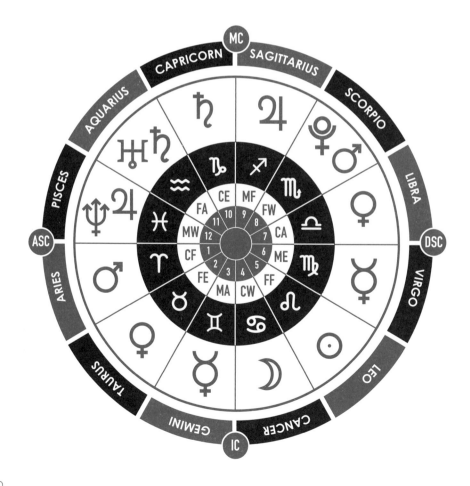

The inside ring identifies the house numbers 1–12.

The next ring out contains double capital letters:
The first capital letter rerpresents the Quadruplicities: Cardinal (C)–Fixed (F)–Mutable (M).
The second capital letter represents the Triplicities: Fire (F)–Earth (E)–Air (A)–Water (W).

The next ring shows the glyphs for the signs; and the next ring, the rulers of those signs.

The outside ring identifies the signs of the zodiac.

On the outside of the ring on the left are the letters ASC, and opposite is the DSC. At the top of the wheel is the MC, and opposite is the IC.

A little explanation is due here:

The letters ASC on the left side of the wheel, as you well know by now, represent your Ascendant or Rising Sign. This is the point that indicates your window on the world, your outlook on life.

Opposite the Ascendant are the letters DSC or the Descendant. The Descendant sits at the cusp of the 7th house of "the other person." This is the house of personal relationships.

At the top of the wheel is the designation MC, or the Midheaven. MC stands for *Medium Coeli* (Latin for the "middle of the sky"). Coeli is pronounced *cheh-lee*. The MC hovers at the 10th house of career position, the point that shows how the world sees you.

Opposite the MC is the IC or *Imum Coeli* (Latin for "bottom of the sky"). The IC resides at the bottom of the chart, at the residence of the 4th house of home, family, and roots.

So there you have it, my friends. This is The Natural Zodiac illustration.

As you continue your studies, you might want to keep a plastic covered copy of this chart handy until you know it thoroughly. This is the framework of astrology, the foundation upon which this incredibly beautiful and insightful art/science is built.

Now, as promised, we're going to peek through your astrological window and eavesdrop on the planets.

CHAPTER TEN
Eavesdropping on the Planets

Are your planets naughty of nice? We're about to find out.

As we explore the connections amongst your planets, do remember my mantra: if there's a problem, blame it on the planets!

You know by now that each of your planets operates through one of the twelve signs in one of the twelve houses. Your planet's sign and house placement is the pure essence of how it wants to act if it were all alone in the world. However, usually the planets are not alone or unaffected by their environment. They live amongst the other planets and the Ascendant, and some of them make connections. And this is when the truth begins to emerge.

Keep in mind that the term "aspects" refers to the connections the planets make to each other and the Ascendant. Those connections are measured in degrees.

Every circle has 360 degrees. The zodiacal circle divided evenly by the 12 signs means each sign contains 30 degrees. I know this is elementary, but I was totally flummoxed by math in grade school. So, I want this to be clear because we will be talking about degrees and the connections between planets in signs.

The number of degrees between planets show the ease or difficulty the planets have communicating with one another. Are your planets friends…do they play and work well together, casually playing toss and enjoying the creative flow? Or are they enemies, squaring off or opposing each other, disagreeing and fighting over who carries the ball?

If things are going well in your life, by all means take the credit. But if you run into major roadblocks, you know who to blame.

Let's find out how your planets talk to each other.

This book will cover the five classic connections, called the **Ptolemaic aspects**.[1] If you want to know more about the Ptolemaic aspects, turn to the endnotes at the back of this book. You really don't need to know that now…but just in case you're curious.

Just as you did for the planets and signs, learn the symbols for each of the five aspects that follow.

| Conjunction | Sextile | Square | Trine | Opposition |

As you become more involved in astrology, you may want to expand into other aspects. However, I have found these five aspects have served me well these many years. I find that too many aspects and asteroids and celestial points in space added to a chart dilute my focus. I realize and respect that other astrologers may find these added points in the chart informative.

In the future, do what is comfortable for you but, for now, please focus on these five aspects: conjunction, sextile, square, trine, and opposition.

Remember that aspects will connect planets in their signs in their houses with other planets in their signs in their houses, if both are in the same degree range.

The closer the aspect between the planets, the more powerful that aspect is. If the aspect is too wide, that aspect has less power.

As you proceed through this section, you may find that some of the sentences sound a bit awkward. Again, they are purposely constructed in this manner in order to define the planetary influences more clearly. Sounds like an oxymoron, but it works.

We'll use Helen's chart throughout this chapter as an example.

BUT FIRST . . . again, not shouting, just getting your attention . . . let's look at the grid at the bottom left of Helen's wheel on page 125 which shows the aspects between the planets. When you know how to read this grid, you will be able to pick out the aspects in the blink of an eye. Isn't it great to be bilingual!

Use the following instructions on how to read Helen's grid.

Ignore the planets listed vertically on the left side of the grid, on the outside. We are working with the planets on the right slanted side of the grid. Picture the planets sitting on the front steps, waiting for you to visit.

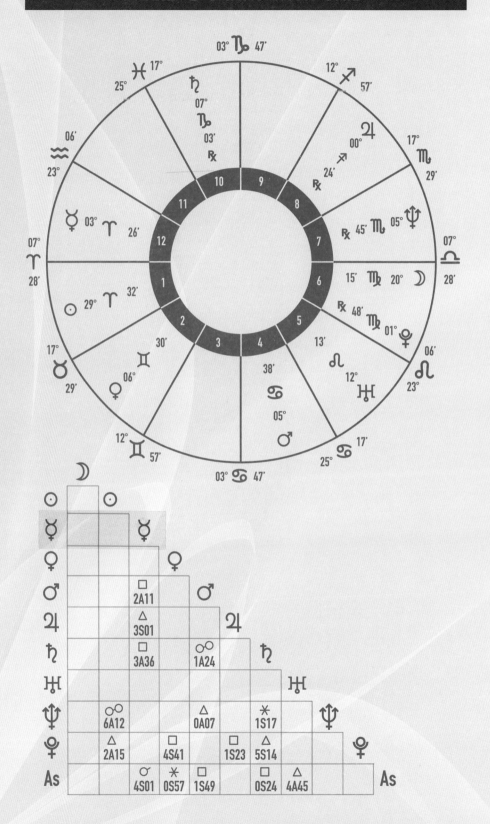

Start with any one of the planets on the right side of the grid, then follow down that column until you come to an aspect. From that point, move all the way to the right to find another planet. Those two planets are in aspect to each other; the symbol will tell you what the aspect is. Ignore the numbers in the blocks for now.

There may be more than one aspect symbol under your planet, which means that planet is talking to more than one other planet. If there are no aspects under a planet, this means the planet expresses on it own, without needing to consult another planet.

Do practice reading your grid a few times before you move on so that you are familiar with the process and thoroughly understand how it works. It will make picking out your aspects so much easier if you do.

Have you done that? Seriously?

All right then, let's move on to discuss the five Ptolemaic aspects.

The Conjunction
Exact: 0 degrees (+/-)

When two or more planets, or planets and the Ascendant, are conjunct, they are close together.

Some astrologers consider the conjunction the most powerful of all the aspects because the planets are tied, and one cannot work without the other. Because they must work together, they have to combine their energies.

Using Helen's chart, look for Helen's Mercury sitting on the steps on the right side of the grid. Follow that Mercury down to the very bottom of the column. There you will find the conjunction symbol. Then look all the way to the right and you will see AS, which is the Ascendant. This means that her Mercury is conjunct her Ascendant.

Her Mercury is in Aries and her Ascendant is in Aries. They work together through the sign Aries. This means she has a quick intelligent mind (Mercury in Aries) and notices everything that comes across her path on a daily basis (Ascendant). She tends to speak (Mercury) quickly (Aries) and sometimes without thinking. Her ideas (Mercury) can break new paths (Aries).

A very important conjunction is that of the Sun and Mercury. You can determine if the person with whom you are communicating will be intellectually sensitive—or more objective—by looking at her Sun/Mercury connection. This awareness can defuse conversations that could potentially turn contentious.

Because Mercury lies between the Earth and the Sun in our solar system, from our Earth point of view, Mercury is always within 28 degrees of the Sun. Remember, in the introduction, astrology is a geocentric or earth centered view of the positions of the planets.

If your Sun and Mercury are conjunct, or close together, your ego, your identity (the Sun) is closely tied to the way you communicate and process information (Mercury). This means that if you make a statement and someone says, "That's a stupid idea," you take their response to mean "you are stupid." You see that as an attack on you personally because you cannot separate who you are (the Sun) from how you think (Mercury). You are your thoughts.

The Sun/Mercury conjunction has a positive side in that you put the full force of yourself into what you have to say; you can inspire others as a teacher, motivator, someone who can initiate change by the power of the Sun behind your words.

If your Sun and Mercury are not conjunct, if they are not close together, your thought process (Mercury) is separated from your identity (the Sun) so that when someone responds to your suggestion with, "That's a stupid idea," you don't take offense. Rather, you might say, "Well, here's another idea." Your thoughts are not connected to your ego. You can handle the comments of others in a more detached way; you think objectively.

When your Sun and Mercury make no aspect to each other, you are more effective in relationships, as a friend, mediator, judge, and in sales and arbitration.

Look at your grid. If you have conjunctions, write a few sentences in your notebook about how the planets and/or the Ascendant work in tandem. Write and maybe rewrite them as ideas circulate in your mind.

Examples of conjunctions:

Sun conjunct Mercury:
Maxwell expresses his identity through the way he communicates. He takes criticism personally.

The same sentence explained:
Maxwell expresses his identity (the Sun) through the way he communicates (Mercury). He takes criticism personally (the Sun conjunct Mercury).

Now we'll add the sign position.

Sun in Sagittarius conjunct Mercury in Sagittarius:
Maxwell expresses his identity enthusiastically and directly through the way he communicates. He takes criticism personally.

The same sentence explained:
Maxwell expresses his identity (the Sun) enthusiastically and directly (Sagittarius) through the way he communicates (Mercury). He takes criticism personally (the Sun conjunct Mercury).

Now, add the house position.

Sun in Sagittarius in the 6th house conjunct Mercury in
Sagittarius in the 6th house:
Maxwell expresses his ego and identity enthusiastically and directly through the way he communicates in his workplace. He takes criticism about his work personally.

The same sentence explained:
Maxwell expresses his ego and identity (the Sun) enthusiastically and directly (Sagittarius) through the way he communicates (Mercury) in his workplace (6th house). He takes criticism about his work (6th house) personally (the Sun conjunct Mercury).

....

Another example:

Mercury conjunct Mars
Elaine speaks assertively and sometimes impatiently.

The same sentence explained:
Elaine speaks (Mercury) assertively and sometimes impatiently (Mars).

Now we'll add the sign. Remember, the conjunction means the planets are together.

Mercury in Capricorn conjunct Mars in Capricorn.
Elaine speaks assertively and sometimes impatiently but always with authority. She is extremely well organized.

The same sentences explained:
Elaine speaks (Mercury) assertively and sometimes impatiently (Mars) but always with authority (Capricorn). She is extremely organized (Mars in Capricorn).

*Mercury in Capricorn in the 8th house conjunct Mars in
Capricorn in the 8th house*

Elaine speaks assertively and sometimes impatiently but with well tested authority.
She is extremely organized when it comes to protecting the well being of those in
her care, whether it is financial or emotional.

The same sentences explained:

Elaine speaks (Mercury) assertively and sometimes impatiently (Mars) but with well
tested authority (Capricorn). She is extremely organized (Mars in Capricorn) when
it comes to protecting the well being of those in her care, whether it is financial or
emotional (the 8th house).

With the conjunctions, when planets are close together, think about how the energy
of each planet works with the energy of the other planet. Use your Sentencing Sheet
and the key words to write sentences about conjunctions in your chart and in the
chart of others.

Practice . . . practice . . . practice.

Which brings to mind another story. After playing a particularly enchanting sonata,
Beethoven was approached by a woman who gushed, "I wish I were as talented as
you, sir." To which Beethoven responded, "Madam. If you practiced eighteen hours
a day for thirty years, you would be just as talented as I am."

I doubt that . . . but the point is well taken.

Practice!

....

The Sextile
Exact: 60 degrees (+/-)

When planets are sextile to one another, they are 60 degrees (or two signs) apart.

The sextile is called an opportunity aspect. It requires actively opening a friendly,
intelligent, and flexible dialogue between the planets involved. In this manner,
opportunities arise that help you achieve the goals designated by these connections.
In other words, the sextile denotes easy discussions that help you achieve your goals.

Go to your grid. You did study it back when I asked you to, right? Good, now that
you know how to work with it, find the sextiles in you chart.

In Helen's chart, find the Saturn symbol on the right side of the grid, follow it down
until you see the sextile. Go all the way to the right and you'll see Neptune. Helen
has Saturn sextile Neptune.

Saturn sextile Neptune:
Helen has the ability to apply her imagination in practical, grounded endeavors. An interest in life's hidden mysteries and her psychic impressions of people suggest she can actively carry on dialogues one-on-one with people in authority who can help her.

The same sentences explained:
Helen has the ability to apply her imagination (Neptune) in practical, grounded endeavors (Saturn in Capricorn). An interest in life's hidden mysteries (Neptune/Scorpio) and her psychic impressions of people (Neptune/7th house), suggest she can actively carry on dialogues (sextile) one-on-one with people (7th house) in authority (Capricorn/10th house) who can help her.

If this character analysis seems complicated, remember it takes time to work through the aspect, planets, signs, and houses. You'll get there, I promise.

So, if you have sextiles in your grid, write sentences about them. Think about your sentences then rework them. You may be able to refine them even further.

Practice . . . practice . . . practice.

To repeat: the sextile is an opportunity aspect. It requires actively opening a friendly, intelligent, and flexible dialogue between the planets involved. This dialogue opens opportunities that help to achieve goals designated by these connections.

Moon sextile Venus
Maureen expresses her emotions by actively engaging in friendly, intelligent dialogue in loving social relations with people. Her imagination speaks to her artistic ability.

The same sentence explained:
Maureen expresses her emotions (the Moon) by actively engaging in friendly, intelligent dialogue (sextile) in loving social relations with people (Venus). Her imagination (the Moon) speaks to her artistic ability (Venus).

Moon in Aquarius sextile Venus in Sagittarius
Maureen expresses her emotions in a detached and open-minded way that allows friendly, intelligent dialogue with people in a loving, positive, and exuberant manner.

The same sentence explained:
Maureen expresses her emotions (the Moon) in a detached and open-minded way (Aquarius) that allows friendly, intelligent dialogue (sextile) with people in a loving (Venus), positive, and exuberant manner (Sagittarius).

Now we'll add the houses in which these two planets are found.

Moon in Aquarius in the 11th house sextile Venus in Sagittarius in the 9th house
Maureen expresses her emotions in a detached and open-minded way through getting involved with groups and humanitarian ventures. This allows her the opportunity to open friendly, intelligent dialogues where she can express her love through such avenues as higher education, publishing, foreign contacts, and travel, all in a positive and exuberant manner.

The same sentence explained:
Maureen expresses her emotions (the Moon) in a detached and open-minded way (Aquarius) through getting involved with groups and humanitarian ventures (11th house). This allows her the opportunity to open friendly, intelligent dialogues (sextile) where she express her love through such avenues as higher education, publishing, foreign contacts, and travel (9th house), all in a positive and exuberant manner (Sagittarius).

....

You see how that works?

Do read it a few times and you will see how it works. Remember, even though some of the sentences may sound stilted, they are still accurate.

Keep in mind that the analysis of the aspects in the chart is one step at a time.

Don't let it make you crazy. If you've seen the old reruns of the Three Stooges, you'll recall when one of them got crazy, with a wild look in his eyes he would say, "Slowly he turned, and step-by-step, inch-by-inch . . . " Astrology is complex so you have to take it slowly, step-by-step, and sometimes even inch-by-inch. Please don't go all wild-eyed on me. Just read the definitions a few times until they begin to make sense.

Let's try another one.

Reminder: The sextile requires actively opening a friendly, intelligent, and flexible dialogue between the planets. In this manner, opportunities arise to achieve goals designated by these connections. (We learn through repetition!)

Mercury sextile Uranus
By actively opening a friendly, intelligent, and flexible dialogue, Matthew can develop his mental capabilities through intuition and inventive avenues. This will provide more opportunities to grow and reach his goals.

The same sentence explained:
By actively opening a friendly, intelligent, and flexible dialogue (sextile), Matthew can develop his mental capabilities (Mercury) through intuition and inventive (Uranus) avenues. This will provide more opportunities (sextile) to grow and reach his goals.

Add the sign positions…

Mercury in Scorpio sextile Uranus in Virgo
By actively opening a friendly, intelligent, and flexible dialogue, Matthew can develop his deep investigative mental capabilities through intuitive and inventive practical applications. This will provide more opportunities to grow and reach his goals.

The same sentence explained:
By actively opening a friendly, intelligent, and flexible dialogue (sextile), Matthew can develop his deep investigative (Scorpio) mental capabilities (Mercury) through intuitive and inventive (Uranus) practical applications (Virgo). This will provide more opportunities to grow and reach his goals.

Add house positions…

Mercury in Scorpio in the 10th house sextile Uranus in Virgo in the 8th house

By actively opening a friendly, intelligent, and flexible dialogue, Matthew can develop his deep investigative mental capabilities in his choice of career through intuitive and inventive practical applications in the fields of finance, medicine, therapy, or metaphysics. This will provide more opportunities to grow and reach his goals.

The same sentence explained:
By actively opening a friendly, intelligent, and flexible dialogue (sextile), Matthew can develop his deep investigative (Scorpio) mental capabilities (Mercury) in his choice of career (10th house) through intuitive and inventive (Uranus) practical applications (Virgo) in the fields of finance, medicine, therapy, or metaphysics (8th house). This will provide more opportunities (sextile) to grow and reach his goals

The sextile aspect requires that you put some effort into the opportunities offered between the planets involved. Use your Sentencing Sheet and the key words to write sentences in your notebook about sextiles between a few of the planets. Practice.

When that is done, you probably need a break so why not put this book down, get up and stretch, do a few gentle rolls of the head and shoulders. Take a nap. Let all these sentences play around in your head.

When you are rested, and your head is clear, we'll move on…

....

The Square
Exact: 90 degrees (+/-)

When a planet is separated by approximately 90 degrees from another planet, the two have problems talking to each other.

The key words for the square are challenge and stress.

So . . . let's eat.

Imagine that you've arranged a dinner party. Your rectangular dining table is quite long. You sit on the long side across from one guest who is directly opposite you on the other side; you are the dark circle. The other four guests are seated at the short sides, two at each end, some distance from you. Please see the seating plan that follows.

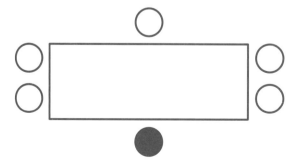

I know you're saying this is an awkward seating arrangement but I'm an astrologer, and I see the world differently. Hopefully, you will too at some point. So bear with me for a moment. Dessert is on its way.

With this arrangement, you can clearly see that one person directly across the table from you. However, the two guests at either end of this long table are not in your line of sight. In fact, they're seated far enough away from you that their conversation is muffled so you can't hear everything they're saying. If you do hear some of it, you're liable to misinterpret what they're saying. This can be irritating. But this is your dinner party, and you set the table. (It's your chart.)

This is the nature of the square. You are not consciously aware of the side conversations carried on by your squares because you are focused on where you are seated. You think the behavior of those guests at the far ends of the table is totally out of line. You can see that squares can be confusing. There is a lack of clarity; you don't quite catch the full-blown conversation, so you misinterpret parts of it.

As a result, you tend to project your irritation on to your guests; however, these people are aspects of yourself. Actually, the behavior that irritates you most in other people is merely unaddressed aspects of your own personality. It's called projection.

Squares are stressful and challenging. They represent irritations that provoke situations, causing friction. When you address these challenges, they become your strengths. The strongest individuals have learned to work out the tension in their squares.

Dessert arrives when you figure this out, and use the awareness to nurture your growth.

Yes, the square is a challenge because a planet square to another planet is operating on a totally different frequency; therefore, they don't understand each other.

If you flex your Quads, you can easily pick out your squares; that's if you learned your Quadruplicities in the last chapter.

Back then, we talked about your action meter, your get-up-and-go, through your planetary placements in the Quadruplicities of Cardinal, Fixed, and Mutable.

You learned why planets in the Cardinal Signs have difficulty getting along with planets in other Cardinal Signs, just as planets in Fixed Signs have difficulty getting along with planets in other Fixed Signs, and why planets in Mutable Signs have difficulty getting along with planets in other Mutable Signs. It's because, in each case, they behave differently.

In the case of the square, we are talking about a 90-degree separation.

Let's take the example of Mars square (in stress position) to Saturn, using the illustrations below. You learned these categories in chapter 8:

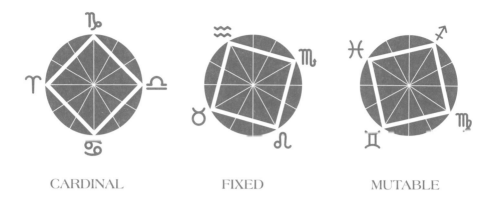

CARDINAL   FIXED   MUTABLE

In the Cardinal Quadruplicity shown, if Mars is in Aries, it is square to Saturn in either Cancer or Capricorn. The same is true if Mars is in Cancer; it is square to Saturn in either Aries or Libra. And so on.

In the Fixed Quadruplicity shown above, if Mars is in Scorpio, it is square to Saturn in either Leo or Aquarius. If Mars is in Taurus, it is square to Saturn in either Aquarius or Leo. And so on.

In the Mutable Quadruplicity shown above, if Mars is in Virgo, it is square to Saturn in either Gemini or Sagittarius. If Mars is in Pisces, it is square to Saturn in either Gemini or Sagittarius.

Mars square Saturn in any one of the three Quadruplicities has difficulty getting along because the two planets operate on different wave lengths. They have nothing in common.

I could go on all day, but now you're mumbling that I already told you that in the last chapter, but as I said, I repeat myself for a purpose. It's that mommy thing again.

When you find a planet 90 degrees from another planet, their action meters are incompatible. There. That's pretty succinct.

When you recognize your squares, and use the positive attributes of each side with awareness, they become your strengths. More about that later.

Go to Helen's grid.

In Helen's chart, you'll find that she has quite a few squares. For practice, you can take any one of them and write a sentence.

But perhaps you'd rather work on your own squares. Look at the grid in your chart.

Find the planets involved and, in your notebook, write a sentence about how you work out those challenges in the way you behave, through your action meter, through how you act.

Let's look at a few examples of squares:

Mercury square Saturn
Communication is stressful for Alexander when he speaks to anyone he perceives as an authority figure.

The same sentence explained:
Communication (Mercury) is stressful (square) for Alexander when he speaks (Mercury) to anyone he perceives as an authority figure (Saturn).

Add sign positions…

Mercury in Leo square Saturn in Taurus
Communication is stressful for Alexander when he tries to speak with confidence to anyone he perceives as a well grounded, financially comfortable authority figure.

The same sentence explained:
Communication (Mercury) is stressful (square) for Alexander when he tries to speak with confidence (Leo) to anyone he perceives as a well grounded, financially comfortable (Taurus) authority figure (Saturn).

Add house positions…

Mercury in Leo in the 6th house square Saturn in Taurus in the 3rd house
Communication is stressful for Alexander when he tries to speak with confidence to anyone in his workplace who he perceives as a well grounded, financially comfortable, and well spoken authority figure.

The same sentence explained:
Communication (Mercury) is stressful (square) for Alexander when he tries to speak with confidence (Leo) to anyone in his workplace (6th house) who he perceives as a well grounded, financially comfortable (Taurus), and well spoken (3rd house) authority figure (Saturn).

Another example:

Sun square the Ascendant:
For years, Louise had a conflict between expressing her true self and her daily approach to living her life.

The same sentence explained:
For years, Louise had a conflict (square) between expressing her true self (Sun), and her daily approach (Ascendant) to living her life.

Add signs positions…

Sun in Scorpio square the Ascendant in Leo
For years, Louise had a conflict between expressing her true self intensely, and her sunny, positive daily approach to living her life.

The same sentence explained:
For years, Louise had a conflict (square) between expressing her true self (Sun) intensely (Scorpio) and her sunny, positive (Leo) daily approach (Ascendant) to living her life.

Add house positions…

Sun in Scorpio in the 4th house square the Ascendant in Leo
For years, Louise had a conflict between expressing her true self intensely and privately at home and her sunny, positive daily approach to living her life.

The same sentence explained:
For years, Louise had a conflict (square) between expressing her true self (Sun) intensely and privately (Scorpio) at home (4th house), and her positive, sunny (Leo) daily approach (Ascendant) to living her life.

Once again, look at the squares in your chart and the charts of others you know. Write a few sentences in your notebook using the method above. Maybe even more than a few. Practice makes perfect!

Which reminds me of the old days when a naughty little boy (it was always a boy) was sent to the blackboard with a piece of white chalk to write 100 times: I will not throw spitballs at the girls.

We learn through repetition!

Let's stop here and talk a bit about the powerful squares. They are your best friends!

Yes, the squares in your chart are stress filled and challenging, but they also supply the energy to build character that leads to personal growth. We often become most efficient in the messages contained within our squares; they become our strengths.

By examining the energy and objective of a sign in a square and comparing it to the energy and objective of the sign that squares it, you will see why the two are inharmonious, even though they are each performing their assigned jobs.

Each of the planets involved in the square is doing exactly what they should be doing.

We have to untangle the web the planets weave around each other. Remember the seating arrangement at the dinner table. We cannot hear the conversations clearly from our position at the table, so we tend to misinterpret those messages.

There should be no finger pointing when you are working with someone who has signs that square yours, rather you should try to understand each other, and then work out a plan that allows each of you to do your own thing with moderation.

I know . . . once again . . . if everyone handled their lives the way we do, the world would be filled with sweet smelling flowers and chocolate bonbons.

Let's examine the previous example where Louise's Scorpio Sun in the hidden and private 4th house is square her outgoing Leo Ascendant. For years, Louise viewed people who were outgoing, friendly, and the life of the party as show-offs, people who wanted to be the center of attention. She saw this in the behavior of anyone who showed the least bit of pizzazz or drama. Because she had not recognized this behavior as part of her own personality, she was projecting her Leo Ascendant on to others.

As I said, squares need individual attention. When counseling this woman, I suggested that she spend individual time with both her Scorpio Sun sign and her Leo Ascendant.

She should spend an allotted period of time in the privacy of her home where she can investigate and dig, whether it is in the garden or through her extensive library, and not allow any interruptions.

When this side of her is fulfilled, she then needs to see what's going on in the world, step out and have some fun outside her home with family and friends, and do things that entertain her, where her Leo Ascendant can shine. She needs to be that person she thought was showing off.

This suggestion worked beautifully for her. She is now comfortable in both roles because she takes care of them separately and for allotted periods of time.

When addressing squares with my clients, I tell them to post a notice on their private door that says, "Do Not Disturb . . . unless there is a Supernova." Then it won't matter anyway. In other words, don't let anything interfere with this process of allotting time for each side of the square. When you are fully engrossed in working on one behavioral aspect of the square, you can comfortably stay with it, knowing that you have another block of time coming up to work on the other seemingly conflicting behavior. Don't let one side bleed into the other. That's when the problems arise.

A square is like riding a car on square wheels. After a while, you take notice of the continuous bumps in your life (the squares) and, at some point, you decide its time to do something about the condition of your tires.

Always embrace your squares. They are character builders and will become your friends. As mentioned above, more often than not, those areas where your squares are prominent will become avenues towards achievement, and may well become the vocation or avocation for which you will be known.

Once again regarding the squares in your chart: think about how the energy of each planet works. Then give each side of your square allotted periods of time when you can express those qualities. Make that time sacred; don't let others pull you away from that activity. Each side of your square deserves your undivided attention.

A Note about a square in my chart:
Years ago, I was sitting out on the deck on a summer's day when I wanted to show my son-in-law an article in a magazine I was reading. I called to him, "Rich, I want you to come here to see this." He smiled and said, "What if I don't want to come there?"

I stopped, suddenly realizing what I had meant as a request sounded more like a demand. The more I thought about it, the more I realized how frequently I used "I want . . ." when requesting something. In that moment of clarity, I learned how much that was ingrained in my thought process. My Mercury (how I think and communicate) is in Scorpio (intense, and yes, sometimes controlling) square (challenging) my Ascendant (my daily approach to life).

My son-in-law taught me a big lesson. Since then, I now say . . . "Would you come here for a minute?" It gives the other person options. And it works a lot better. So, I have learned over my many years on this planet to moderate that intensity; rather, I use it in the appropriate manner like researching for this book, and in the articles and books I have written, and the research and preparation for my classes.

Again, use your Sentencing Sheet and a few keys words to write as many sentences as you want about planets in square to each other.

The Trine
Exact: 120 degrees (+/-)

A trine is when planets, or planets and the Ascendant, are 120 degrees apart.

On the illustration of The Natural Zodiac, signs that are 120 degrees (or three signs apart) are trine to each other. Remember the Triplicities? The signs shown in the Triplicities illustrations are connected by triangles, and they are trine to each other. They flow easily into each other because they are in the same Elements. The energy of planets in Fire signs easily flow from one to the other. The same is true of the planets in Earth signs, the planets in Air signs, and the planets in Water signs.

There is no friction with the trine; nothing stopping the flow. That can be good or not so good, as we shall see.

Where the sextile is an aspect of opportunity because there is energy expended in reaching out to accomplish something, the trine is just there—"been there, done that" sort of attitude.

Because the energy of the trines flows so easily, there are three things that can happen.

1. You spend your summer lazily swinging in the hammock with an iced glass of lemonade in hand, enjoying the flow of the planets in trine, lazily humming a soothing summer song.
2. You can overlook your trines because you find them so easy to perform that you fall asleep in that hammock. You don't often notice them, and you don't place any value upon them. You think everyone can do what you do so easily.
3. Or you can use them! What a novel concept!

As mentioned in the introduction, you came in with a spiritual bankbook with credits and debits. Trines are your credits; don't overlook them. Use them when you need to get out of jams with some conjunctions, and with your squares and oppositions (the opposition aspect is coming shortly).

The trine energy is easy, flowing, creative, and can be advantageous. Others may see this as a talent you have, although you may not initially recognize it as such because it comes so easily to you.

The trines can be easily found by looking, once again, at the illustrations of the Triplicities pictured below, shown here so you don't have to flip back and forth while reading these examples.

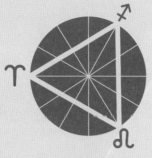

FIRE

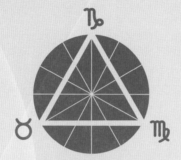

EARTH

AIR

WATER

Here are a few examples of trines.

Mars trine Jupiter
A professional organizer, Sarah takes on big jobs, knowing she can handle them with ease.

The same sentence explained:
A professional organizer, Sarah takes on big jobs (Jupiter), knowing she can handle them (Mars) with ease (trine).

Add signs…

Mars in Virgo trine Jupiter in Capricorn
A professional organizer, Sarah takes on big jobs with a serious professional attitude, knowing she can easily handle them with efficient precision and an eye to detail.

The same sentence explained:
A professional organizer, Sarah takes on big jobs (Jupiter) with a serious professional attitude (Capricorn), knowing she can easily (trine) handle them (Mars) with efficient precision and an eye to detail (Virgo).

Add houses...

Mars in Virgo in the 4th house trine Jupiter in Capricorn in the 8th house
A professional organizer, Sarah takes on big jobs that generate a healthy income with a serious, cautious attitude, knowing she can easily handle them with efficient precision and an eye to detail as she works on the plans at her home office.

The same sentence explained:
A professional organizer, Sarah takes on big jobs (Jupiter) that generate a healthy income (8th house) with a serious, cautious attitude (Capricorn), knowing she can easily (trine) handle them (Mars) with efficient precision and an eye to detail (Virgo) as she works on the plans at her home office (4th house).

Sarah did come to recognize that not everyone can handle big projects as easily as she can, so she learned to charge for her "talent" rather than give it away.

Is this process working for you? As I mentioned, the sentences may sound awkward, but they were written in this manner so you could see how the planets describe the actions.

Here's another example:

Venus trine Uranus
For Nicholas, romance and beauty flow easily and are filled with excitement and the unusual.

The same sentence explained:
For Nicholas, romance and beauty (Venus) flow easily (trine) and are filled with excitement and the unusual (Uranus).

Add signs . . .

Venus in Gemini trine Uranus in Libra
For Nicholas, romance and beauty expressed cleverly and with variety flows easily and are filled with excitement and the unusual in a pleasing relationship-oriented manner.

The same sentence explained:
For Nicholas, romance and beauty (Venus) expressed cleverly and with variety (Gemini) flows easily (trine) and are filled with excitement and the unusual (Uranus) in a pleasing relationship-oriented manner (Libra).

Add houses . . .

Venus in Gemini in the 3rd house trine Uranus in Libra in the 10th house
For Nicholas, romance and beauty expressed cleverly and with variety through his writing and speaking flows easily and is filled with excitement and the unusual in a pleasing relationship-oriented manner in his career.

The same sentence explained:
For Nicholas, romance and beauty (Venus) expressed cleverly and with variety (Gemini) through his writing and speaking (3rd house) flows easily (trine) and is filled with excitement and the unusual (Uranus) in a pleasing relationship-oriented manner (Libra) in his career (10th house).

Nicholas is a poet as well as a verse contributor to the romantic department of a greeting card company. He always had a knack for expressing his romantic feelings (ask his wife!). One day after much prodding from her, he submitted and sold some of his verse, and went on from there to earn much of his income from his "natural" ability. He might have overlooked his ability had it not been for his wife insisting that he use it productively.

With your trines, think about how the energy of one planet flows with the energy of the other planet.

You can use your Sentencing Sheet and key words to write a few sentences in your notebook about any trines in your chart or the charts of family, friends, and so forth. And make up a few sentences; you don't have to tell them.

Well, actually, write more than a few sentences. Practice . . . practice . . . practice.

Need another break? Please take one—I know I need one. I'll be back in a few minutes.

I'm back . . . we're now on to the oppositions.

The Opposition
Exact: 180 degrees (+/-)

An opposition occurs when planets, or planets and the Ascendant, are exactly opposite each other in the chart. This means they are 180 degrees apart, or half the circle. Oppositions mean exactly that; the two opposing planets or planets and the Ascendant have two opposing points of view.

Oppositions are easy to pick out.

Still hungry? Well then, back to the dinner table.

It's another evening and you're entertaining another group of friends at your long dinner table. But you have rearranged the seating plan. Now, you are sitting at the short side directly opposite the person at the far end of the table; the dark circle marks your spot. Your other four guests are seated on the long sides, two on each side. See the seating plan that follows.

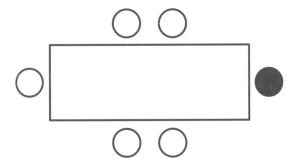

You can clearly see the person sitting opposite you. However, you and this person are farther apart than the other occupants at the table so you have to speak loudly. You should keep the shouting to a minimum when you and the guest opposite you engage in back and forth exchanges.

Your dialogue is obvious. Everyone at the table can hear you both. You espouse one point of view; she states a different point of view.

Opposing points of view are obvious and require compromise. In order to avoid conflict, there must be a coming together in order to bring about a peaceful resolution that will satisfy both sides.

In the astrological chart, two planets in opposition are as far away as they can possibly be in the wheel. 180 degrees divides the wheel in half. The art of compromise is essential.

Oppositions are obvious; they work out through relationships. Relationships require compromise and balance between two extremes. One side of the opposition feels separated from the other side; therefore, we seek out methods to help us find a balance between the uncertainties caused by the seesaw effect of this aspect. One moment, one side of our seesaw is elevated and noticeable; the next minute that expression sinks to the lower level while the other sides rise for recognition. So, which side are we on?

The opposition is worked out through interaction with others, through one-on-one relationships, where we become aware of the inconsistencies in our behavior. We then learn to be good negotiators between the two planets, finding a middle ground, a compromise, where they can both exist.

Go to the grid in Helen's chart.

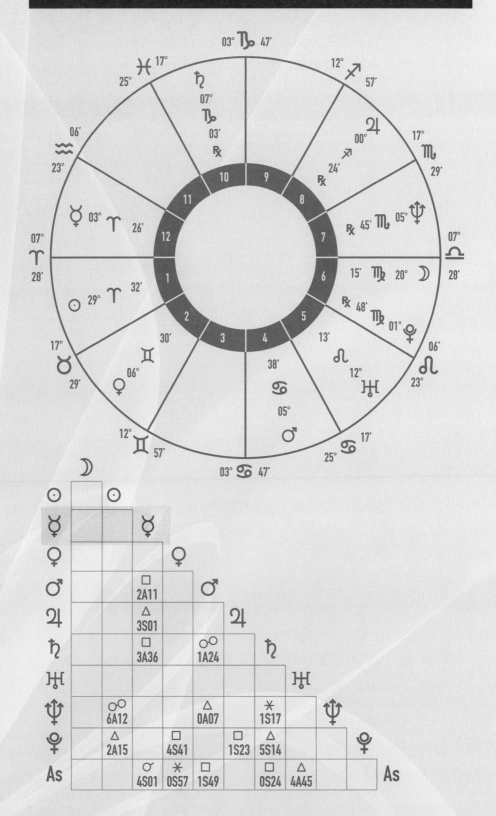

In Helen's chart, she has the:

Sun opposite Neptune
Helen has to be careful that others don't drain her energy. Also, she must not sacrifice her own identity for others by giving too much.

The same sentence explained:
Helen has to be careful that others (opposition) don't drain her energy (Neptune). Also, she must not sacrifice her own identity (the Sun) for others by giving too much (Neptune).

Add signs…

Sun in Aries opposite Neptune in Scorpio:
Helen has to be careful that others who try to control her don't drain her energy. Also, she must not sacrifice her own dynamic identity.

The same sentence explained:
Helen has to be careful that others (opposition) who try to control her (Scorpio) don't drain her energy (Neptune). Also, she must not sacrifice (Neptune) her own dynamic identity (Sun in Aries).

Sun in Aries in H1 opposite Neptune in Scorpio in H7:
Helen has to be careful that others who try to control her in personal relationships don't drain her dynamic energy. Also, she must not sacrifice her own identity for a mate.

The same sentence explained:
Helen has to be careful that others who try to control her (Scorpio) in personal relationships (H7) don't drain (Neptune) her dynamic energy (Sun in Aries). Also, she must not sacrifice (Neptune) her own identity (the Sun) for a mate (H7).

(A note about Helen's opposition for those of you who might have noticed. Her Sun is at the last degree of Aries, and her Neptune is at the beginning of Scorpio. These two signs are not opposite; however, because they are so close in degree, this is called an out-of-sign or dissociate opposition. If you don't know what I'm talking about, don't worry about it. It's not important at this point in your lessons.)

Look at your grid. If you have oppositions, write a number of sentences in your notebook describing how your oppositions work out in your life.

A few more examples:

Sun opposite Uranus
When Louie expresses his ego, he evokes negative responses from others because of his eccentricity. He needs to be free to express his individuality even though that expression may change from day to day. He must learn to compromise his ego expression when he's relating to other people.

The same sentence explained:
When Louie expresses his ego (the Sun), he evokes negative responses from others (opposition) because of his eccentricity (Uranus). He needs to be free (Uranus) to express his individuality (the Sun) even though that expression may change (Uranus) from day to day. He must learn to compromise (opposition) his ego expression (the Sun) when he's relating to other people (opposition).

Add signs…

Sun in Gemini opposite Uranus in Sagittarius
When Louie expresses his ego intellectually, he evokes negative responses from others because of his outspoken eccentricities. He needs to be free to express his individuality, even though that expression may change from day to day. He must learn to compromise his ego expression when relating to others.

The same sentence explained:
When Louie expresses his ego (the Sun) intellectually (Gemini), he evokes negative responses from others (opposition) because of his outspoken (Sagittarius) eccentricities (Uranus). He needs to be free (Uranus) to express his individuality, even though that expression may change from day to day. He must learn to compromise (opposition) his ego expression when relating to others.

Add houses…

Sun in Gemini in the 7th house opposite Uranus in
Sagittarius in the 1st house
When Louie expresses his ego intellectually in personal relationships, he evokes negative responses from the other person because of his outspoken and eccentric outlook on life. He needs to be personally free to express his ego, even though that expression may change from day to day. His appearance may be unusual in some way.

The same sentence explained:
When Louie expresses his ego (the Sun) intellectually (Gemini) in personal relationships (7th house), he evokes negative responses from the other person (opposition) because of his outspoken (Sagittarius) and eccentric (Uranus) outlook on life (1st house). He needs to be personally (1st house) free (Uranus) to express his ego (the Sun), even though that expression may change (Uranus) from day to day. His appearance (1st house) may be unusual (Uranus) in some way.

Louie needs to become aware that he must tone down his intellectual ego expression and listen to the opinions of others on occasion. He could find enlightenment in this exchange.

....

One more example:

Moon opposite Venus
Alex is emotionally sensitive. She often feels separated from the love she needs from others. Therefore, she may feed her emotional needs by absorbing sweets and buying personal items.

The same sentence explained:
Alex is emotionally sensitive (the Moon). She often feels separated from (opposition) the love (Venus) she needs from others. Therefore, she may feed her emotional needs (the Moon) by absorbing (the Moon) sweets and buying personal items (Venus).

Add signs to the equation…

Moon in Leo opposite Venus in Aquarius

Alex is emotionally sensitive and she needs recognition. She often feels separated from the love she needs from others, who seem detached. Therefore, she may feed her emotional needs by overindulging in sweets and buying personal items.

The same sentence explained:
Alex is emotionally sensitive (the Moon) and she needs recognition (Leo). She often feels separated from (the opposition) the love (Venus) she needs from others, who seem detached (Aquarius). Therefore, she may feed her emotional needs (the Moon) by absorbing (the Moon) sweets and buying personal items (Venus).

Add houses . . .

Moon in Leo in the 8th house opposite Venus in Aquarius in the 2nd house

Alex is emotionally sensitive and she needs recognition. She wants a deeply committed relationship. She often feels separated from the love she needs from others, who seem detached and more concerned with their own financial pursuits and well-being. Therefore, she may feed her emotional needs by absorbing sweets and buying personal items.

The same sentence explained:
Alex is emotionally sensitive (the Moon) and she needs recognition (Leo). She wants a deeply committed relationship (8th house). She often feels separated from (opposition) the love (Venus) she needs from others, who seem detached (Aquarius) and more concerned with their own financial pursuits and well-being (2nd house). Therefore, she may feed her emotional needs (the Moon) by absorbing (the Moon) sweets and buying personal items (Venus).

With oppositions, you become aware of the balance needed between the energy of the planet on one end of the seesaw and the energy of the planet on the other end of the seesaw. This awareness will work out through negotiations with others to find that balance point.

Use your Sentencing Sheet and key words to write a whole bunch of sentences in your notebook delineating the oppositions in your chart and the oppositions in the charts of family, pets, friends, famous personalities, or any other thing that has a birthday.

Practice makes perfect. Remember Beethoven.

And there you have it. The five Ptolemaic aspects.

Now you can actually read a chart! I am so proud of you!

But please don't stop here. Go back over the chapters until the information contained within this book is like second nature to you.

You are now bi-lingual, as one astrologer put it. You can read in your native language as well as in the language of astrological symbols. As the astrological language becomes more familiar to you, you will become a storyteller who can weave magical stories that will transform the lives of others.

Make the planets your friends; have conversations with them. They are waiting to whisper celestial messages in your ears.

Are you ready for the next step? Well, turn the page…

CHAPTER ELEVEN

Graduation and Dreams

Wow! You've Done It!

You've realized your dream. You've always wanted to become an astrologer . . . right? Well, you're on your way.

You have come to the end of this first instructional phase of your course. If you have followed all the instructions to the letter, the Delphic inscription "Know thyself" is emblazoned in gold letters across your diploma.

As mentioned in the Introduction, you now have your spiritual bankbook marked with credits and debits.

Now that you have the information in this book thoroughly embedded in those marvelous little gray cells of yours, do think about continuing your astrological education. Astrology is a journey that is filled with wonder, delight, and amazement, and it will bring you insights not only into your own life but also into the lives of those you love, and all the other people who will walk into your life. Through understanding differences in how each person approaches life, you can improve your relationships.

But most importantly, astrology offers you a deep, accurate look within yourself. This wonderful art/science sheds light on the truly wonderful being that is you, and proves that:

You are Exactly Who You Should Be!

So, my friends, remember what the poet Browning wrote: "Your reach should exceed your grasp, or what's a heaven for?" Reach for the stars, and keep your cosmic guardians close. They are watching over you.

In the meantime, I'm sending you off with cap and gown into the big wide world to amaze those you touch with your astrological wisdom. Be proud of what you have learned; treat it with respect. And know that one day, with the help of your cosmic guardians, you may have the privilege of guiding others on their starry pathway.

I send you Love, Light, and Laughter, the holy trinity of Life.

A Dream

Please let me share a dream I had when I was finishing this book.

First, a little background.

As is my process when writing a book or an article, I live with it day and night. Literally.

I wake up at 2:30 in the morning thinking, I need to change that word. It will read better. Or, that section isn't quite right. How am I going to fix it? Of course, my cats love it when I trudge sleepily to the sunporch to write. They are night creatures after all. It's just so hard to keep them off my computer keyboard. I've had a few cat-tastrophes so I now cover my keyboard with a makeshift box I taped together when I get up and leave my desk for a few moments.

What was I talking about . . . oh, yes. The book . . .

I think about the book while I'm eating breakfast, usually at my computer along with the cats, and when I'm picking up the house, cleaning the litter boxes, and when I'm trying to watch the baseball game or a mystery on NetFlix.

My Mercury in Scorpio is a blessing and a curse. And Mars and Jupiter in the 6th house of work insist that I dot every "i" and cross every "t". I reread a manuscript more times than I want to admit because it has to be as nearly perfect as possible.

I wear myself out working to make the information in the book (or the article) instructional, flowing, and easy to understand. The greatest compliments I receive are: "Your book is so easy to understand and fun to read."

In true intense Scorpio fashion, I'm glad that the blood, sweat, and tears behind my writing is hidden.

Now, my dream:

As I reached into a dark closet, I see it . . . lurking in the shadows . . . a bushy, healthy green plant about waist high, staring wild-eyed at me. I know that this plant is about to grow rampant, and I need to get it out of the house.

I grab it by the waist but it squirms and twists, like a cat when you try to pick it up. I don't want it to get away from me, so I grasp it by gently the neck, like a mother cat does with her kitten, and carry it outside the house.

My interpretation:

The plant is my book, green and healthy, but still hidden in the closets of my mind. It stares at me with an attitude like: get me out of here. I grasp it around the waist; it squirms and twists, which is my mind trying to get everything in this book in the right order.

Finally, I grasp it gently by the neck (the neck is ruled by Taurus, and Taurus sits on my 10th house of career and public recognition). The book needs to get out to the public. Like a mother cat with her kitten, I have nurtured this book one page at a time so that it will have a life.

And here we are…that plant is now out in the light of the public in the form of this book, hopefully where it will continue to grow through helping those who read it to move on to become future astrologers.

I welcome your feedback about the ways in which I can improve my methods. I also, of course, love hearing the good stuff. You can reach me at www.dustybunker. com or at dustybunker@comcast.net, so please, do drop in.

Now . . . on to dig for gold . . .

CHAPTER TWELVE

The Pot of Gold

As I wrote this book, I found myself interjecting information that seemed helpful at the time but, upon subsequent readings, realized it was distracting from the flow of the book. I feel this information is important enough to include so I decided to gather it together in this chapter. What follows is a collection of astrological nuggets and gems that glow and glitter, and hopefully add more treasure to your education.

A Very, Very Brief History of Astrology:

The timeline of the development of human consciousness in this regard is beyond the scope or the intention of this book. However, a few memorable dates are listed below.

Phases of the Moon seemed to have been recorded in the ancient past.

25,000–10,000 BCE: in a 1964 article in *Science Magazine*, the writer contended that, during this period, nicks cut in reindeer bones and mammoth ivory represent the phases of the Moon.

6000 BCE: the Sumerians began to observe and note the movements in the sky.

3000 BCE: Sargon the Great, ruler of Sumer (now southern Iraq), made astrological predictions.

Around 2200 BCE: the Chaldeans recorded astrological information, including predictions, on clay tablets.

In 70 BCE: the first Greek horoscope using the precise hour of birth was constructed.

In the Hellenic period, over 2,000 years ago: tropical astrology was formalized into what most of the Western world uses today.

An Important Note Here About a Planet in a Sign:

As mentioned at the end of chapter 2, the old systems of astrology designated planets in certain signs as stronger (dignified, exaltation) or weaker (debilitated, in fall). I disagree with these assessments. A planet in a sign just *is*. What you do with it and how you feel about what you do with it determines the success of that planet.

Astrologer Eric Meyers, in his article in the December/January 2015 issue of *The Mountain Astrologer* titled "From Separation to Connection," writes that "all dignities and debilities are entirely meaningless today within a tropical context." He states that the old patriarchal view of the world rewards the Yang male competitive mind-set of "assertiveness, self promotion, and endurance." This view entirely discounts and denigrates the Yin qualities of acceptance, love, gentleness, and support. This is a new age and the Yin is rising! Female qualities are slowly being recognized as equal to male qualities; the two sides just operate differently.

So please don't get caught up in internal conversations like . . . oh no, my Mars is in detriment, I'll never get anything done . . . or my Venus is in its fall, who will ever love me? It's all balderdash. So forget it! You are exactly who you should be and you have all the tools in your astrologic tool box to build the perfect life for yourself.

M and F:
Starting with Aries, each sign is alternately designated as Male and Female. This is not Male and Female in human terms but rather in terms of Active and Reactive.

The old astrology books called these Active (Male) and Passive (Female). There is nothing passive about female energy. I refer you to the Mama Bear syndrome. In today's terms, these are Active and Reactive: the rhythm of life, the ebb and flow, the Yin and Yang.

Cusps and Angles:
The dividing line leading into each house counter-clockwise is the "cusp" of that house. The cusps of 1st, 4th, 7th, and 10th houses are called the angles. You can see that these four points make a cross. The angles indicate you (the Ascendant and the 1st house), your family and base of operations (the 4th house), your relationships (the 7th house) and your career, your home away from home (the 10th house).

Houses:
You may hear the terms Angular, Succedent, and Cadent. These are in some ways similar to the Modalities of Cardinal, Fixed, and Mutable.

The Angular Houses are the 1st, 4th, 7th, and 10th.
The Succedent Houses are the 2nd, 5th, 8th, and 11th.
The Cadent Houses are the 3rd, 6th, 9th, and 12th.

Double initials:
You will find double initials in The Natural Zodiac for each of the signs. These represent the combined designations of the elements—Fire, Earth, Air, and Water—and of the modalities—Cardinal, Fixed, and Mutable.

What these initials mean:

Aries is CF or Cardinal Fire: the most active of the fire sign as opposed to the fixed fire of Leo and the adaptable fire of Sagittarius.

Taurus is FE or Fixed Earth: the most fixed of the Earth signs as opposed to the adaptable Earth of Virgo and the active Earth of Capricorn.

Gemini is MA or Mutable Air: the most adaptable of the Air signs as opposed to the active air of Libra and the Fixed Air of Aquarius.

Cancer is CW or Cardinal Water: the most active of the Water signs as opposed to the Fixed Water of Scorpio and the adaptable Water of Pisces.

And so it goes. Think about what the above brief definitions mean for each sign. Spend time analyzing how the energy of each sign is used, and how each sign is different from the others. No two signs are alike.

Degrees in the Signs:

Every circle has 360 degrees. Dividing the number of degrees in a circle by the twelve signs of the zodiac means each sign contains 30 degrees. Each one degree is also divided into 60 parts called minutes. This is not the same as minutes on the clock.

Therefore, each sign in the zodiac goes from 0 degrees, 0 minutes to 29 degrees, 59 minutes. The next sign starts again at 0 degrees, 0 minutes and goes to 29 degrees, 59 minutes, and so on.

Example: Aries starts at 0 degrees, 0 minutes and ends at 29 degrees 59 minutes. Taurus begins at 0 degrees, 0 minutes and ends at 29 degrees, 59 minutes. Gemini begins at . . . well, you get the picture.

Concerning the Conjunction:

There is a term called dissociate conjunction, or an out-of-sign conjunction. On occasion, you will find a planet at the very end of one sign, say at 28 or 29 degrees, and another planet at 1 or 2 degrees of the following sign. Since there are 30 degrees in a sign, these two are close together. However, these two are considered an out-of-sign, or disassociate, conjunction. It may be less powerful because it brings in the energies of two different signs. For instance, the individual with the Sun at the end of one sign, and Mercury at the very beginning of the next sign, (a dissociate conjunction) may, at times, find it difficult to say exactly what she means.

I use charts drawn to look like the houses are of equal size because it is easier for me to read. However, seldom does a chart have the degrees evenly distributed amongst the twelve houses. You may find a chart where one house contains 44 degrees and another house has only 28 degrees.

If the houses in a chart are drawn true to size or proportional, one house will look larger than the smaller one next to it.

To understand the mathematical mechanics of setting up houses is beyond the scope of this book. Just keep in mind that, as the birthplace you are working with, moves toward the north and south poles, and because of the curvature Earth, some houses are quite big while others shrink considerably.

See the illustrations below keeping in mind that the charts are identical:

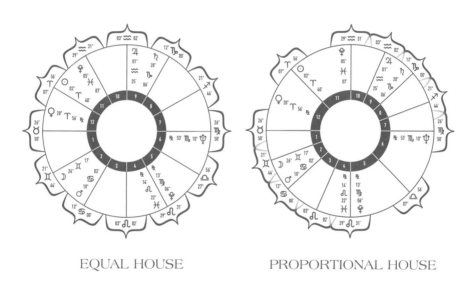

EQUAL HOUSE   PROPORTIONAL HOUSE

The Order of the Planets:

In chapter 1, you were asked to learn the planets in order. They are placed in this order according to their speed through the signs and around the zodiac: the Moon is the fastest, moving through a sign every two to three days; Pluto is the slowest, anywhere from 12–31 years through one sign.

PL as Pluto:

You may occasionally see the initials PL for the sign Pluto. PL is the start of the name Pluto…but the most commonly used symbol is,

The Sun's Position in Your Chart:

By now you know that you need the exact time of day that you were born to determine where your planets are positioned in your chart. The astrological wheel is a twenty-four-hour clock with the Sun as the timekeeper. The wheel turns once every twenty-four hours, pulled by the movement of the Sun in a clockwise direction so that, during one day's time, all twelve signs will eventually be seen rising or ascending.

At sunrise, the Sun will rise from the left side of the chart, somewhere around the 12th and 1st houses, and then continue clockwise to the top of the chart in the vicinity of the 10th house, around noontime. From there it moves to late afternoon/ early evening around the 7th house cusp, descending to the bottom of the chart, around the 4th house near midnight.

So, if you were born around noon, your Sun will be near the top of the wheel; if closer to midnight, it will be near the bottom; if you were born near dawn, you will find the Sun on the left side of the chart around the 1st and 12th houses, and if you were born closer to late afternoon, your Sun will be in the vicinity of the 7th house. These are rough approximations, but you get the idea.

One quick way to determine if your chart corresponds to the time registered on your birth certificate is to note the position of the Sun as explained above.

At a conference some years ago, a woman approached me with her son's chart in hand. She couldn't understand why, with his Sun in the 10th house, he was such a stay-at-home person. Suspecting the time was wrong, I asked what time of day he was born. She said 11:31 p.m. With that time close to midnight, his Sun should be close to the bottom of the chart, probably in the 4th house of the home. Someone had mistakenly entered his birth time as 11:31 a.m. on the computer. With his Sun in the 4th house, he would shine in his home environment.

Full Moons

Full moons make people restless. Those who are sensitive to begin with will feel the effects more strongly and have restless nights. The more steady, fixed individuals might wake themselves up once during the night, snoring, glance out at the moon, then fall back to sleep.

A police detective friend says that during full moons he's actually found people on the beach howling under the lunar influence.

Scientifically, the full moon creates more positive ions, which collect on the skin, making us uneasy. When we take a shower, we wash them off and, as a result, feel refreshed. There are fewer positive ions at higher elevations so when we climb mountains we also have that refreshed elevated feeling (no pun intended).

Full Moons pull on the fluids of the earth, affecting the ocean tides. Since our blood is a fluid, it reacts to the pull of the moon. Hospital reports state that there is more bleeding during the full moon.

More about the Serpent:

Note: I was brought up in a Christian-Judeo society so much of what is explained here is through that lens. You may have a different history and background through which the same ideas have been woven.

In the introduction I talked about the secret taught in the ancient mystery schools: to know (Aquarius); to do (Taurus); to dare (Leo); and to be silent (Scorpio).

The following admonition is found in the Christian Bible, in Matthew 10:16: "Behold, I am sending you out as sheep in the midst of wolves, so be wise as serpents and innocent as doves."

The serpent as wisdom comes from the awareness of the Sun's undulating movement over the Earth's equator in a serpentine fashion. With the passage of time, we are supposed to become wiser, thus the serpent evolved as the symbol of wisdom.

In Christianity, Adam and Eve were nurtured in safety in the Garden of Eden; this might equate to the womb. The serpent (the life force and wisdom) tempted Eve with an apple. An apple has traditionally been associated with knowledge; we give an apple to the teacher. The eating of the apple of knowledge resulted in the couples' expulsion from the womb-like Garden of Eden into life, into the light. The child is now separated from its source and is born into a new existence of knowledge and awareness where it must eventually find its own way. This sounds exactly like the birth process.

The medical symbol, the caduceus, portrays two snakes, symbols of the life force, wound around the staff and up the rod, the spinal cord, elevating the life force to the head, the seat of thought and knowledge, where the wings of flight lift us to higher realms of consciousness.

From ancient Egypt we have the ouroboros, a snake or dragon, depicted in a circle eating its own tail, the alchemical symbol for eternal recycling, the continuous unbroken circle of life. The early Mesoamericans worshipped a deity called Quetzalcoatl, the name means "feathered serpent." Across so many cultures, the snake or dragon symbolizes life, a deep-seated awareness of the serpentine flow of the sun over the equator.

So think twice about trampling those little garter snakes that startle you on the path to the garden or on your walk through the woods; they are the life force energy in disguise. I think of the early American flag depicting a rather nasty looking rattlesnake hovering above the words, Don't Tread On Me—perhaps a message that the enemy should beware of trampling on the life force . . . the knowledge, beliefs, and freedoms of another people

The Light:

The Sun sheds light, lifts us out of darkness into an awareness of our surroundings where we can see. In myths, legends, and in our language, light is a metaphor for knowledge, understanding, and truth. Note the common expressions today: when we finally understand a concept or direction, we might say "I see the light," or "'light dawns." Cartoonists often picture a light bulb over a character's head indicating the birth of an idea or the "I get it" moment. In the Tarot, Key Nine depicts a figure holding the lighted lantern of knowledge to guide others to the mountaintop of elevated consciousness. In the Christian Bible, after God created heaven and earth, He said, "Let there be light . . ." In the 5,000 year old Rig Veda, the world began when a point exploded into light.

Trines, Things in Threes:

The triangle, the first perfect shape that can be drawn with three straight lines, symbolizes the flow of energy. We say "things happen in threes." We live in a three-dimensional world. Note the trinity of mother-father-child in many religions: in Hinduism, Paganism, the Egyptian trinity of Isis, Osiris, and Horus. In Christianity, the trinity is called Father, Son, and Holy Ghost; the Holy Ghost is the Mother. The early patriarchal church fathers tried to eliminate the female from the trinity, but the people wouldn't let go of the mother. Thus we have the Virgin Mary whose statue dominates many homes, yards, and churches around the world.

Three Types of Seekers:

Somewhere I read there are three types of seekers in the world. I sense that this description was attributed to Pythagoras, but I'm not sure where I found it.

1. Novitiates: those who don't know but don't know that they don't know.
2. Initiates: those who don't know but know that they don't know.
3. Illuminati: those who know and know that they know.

The only problem is that sometimes the first group thinks they're the third.

The Earth's Motions:

Our earth has three basic movements: its daily revolution, its yearly circuit around the Sun, and the approximately 26,000 year wobble called the Precession of the Equinoxes.

The daily revolution of approximately 24 hours and the yearly revolution of approximately 365+ days are obvious to us today. But what is this third wobble: the Precession of the Equinoxes? Well, remember the old '60s tune, "When the Sun is in the 7th house and Jupiter aligns with Mars . . . this is the dawning of the Age of Aquarius"? That's what we're about to talk about.

The Precession of the Equinoxes:

While the earth is busy with its daily rotation and yearly circuit on its path around the sun, it also tends to wobble a bit, like a top that is slowing down. Imagine a pen pushed through the earth from the south pole to the north pole, and then imagine a piece of paper at the tip of that pen. After about 26,000 years, that pen will complete one circle on that piece of paper. Since a circle is always 360 degrees and the tip of the pen moves about one degree every 72 years, it takes about 26,000 years to complete one circle.

When we divide this 26,000 year period by the twelve constellations, we find that each constellation covers approximately 2,100 years, which is called an Age. A new age occurs when the vernal equinox points toward the beginning of one of the constellations. Because of the rotation of the earth, these ages move backwards through the constellations.

Each new Age introduces changes in religions, philosophies, cultures, and societal practices reflecting the constellation through which it moves. At the beginning of a new Age, there seems to be events that in retrospect define the direction of that new Age.

Let's briefly examine a few of the Ages past, keeping in mind that each age brings in its opposite sign as well. Again, I will view this from the Judeo-Christian viewpoint.

The Age of Aries (opposite sign Libra)

The Age of Aries covered the time period from about 2100 BCE to the year 0.
Aries is a Fire sign, represented by the ram (or the lamb); its opposite sign is Libra. At the beginning of the Age of Aries, Moses came down off the mountaintop with the Ten Commandments, one in each arm, the Libra scales of justice. He admonished the people for worshipping the golden calf (the bull) because the previous 2,100 year period called the Age of Taurus (whose symbol is the bull) was over. The rituals and initiations were now to be performed by Fire (Aries) and the sacrifice of lambs (the symbol of Aries, the Ram). The two tablets (the scales of justice, Libra) containing the Ten Commandments became the law.

The Age of Pisces (opposite sign Virgo)

The Age of Pisces began around the year 0 to about 2100 ACE.
We experienced and are still finishing the rituals of the Age of Pisces and its opposite sign Virgo. Pisces, the sign of the fish, is a Water sign. At the beginning of the Piscean Age, persecuted Christians drew the sign of the fish to alert others of similar faith. The rituals include baptism in water (Pisces), and the use of the sacraments of bread and wine (the harvest of Virgo) as symbols of the body of Christ.

The Age of Pisces is/was an age of spirituality, caring about and helping the poor and the suffering. It was about sacrifice, the giving away of one's worldly goods for the benefit of the masses. Inscribed on the base of the Statue of Liberty in New York harbor are the immortal words written by poet Emma Lazarus:

> Give me your tired, your poor,
> Your huddled masses yearning to breathe free,
> The wretched refuse of your teeming shore.
> Send these, the homeless, tempest-tossed, to me:
> I lift my lamp beside the golden door.

The Age of Aquarius (opposite sign Leo)

We are living on the cusp of the new 2,100 year Age of Aquarius.

Aquarius, an Air sign, and its opposite sign, Leo, a Fire sign, are the focus of the next 2,100 years. The late astrologer Jeff Jawer joked that Aquarians love humanity; it's the people they have a problem with. Aquarius represents the free exchange of information (Aquarius) through air waves that fire up and liberate the creativity of the individual (Leo). The universal exchange of information with the invention of computers and the Internet reflects the message of Aquarius. Small groups of people (Aquarius) gather to worship in their own independent ways, with no need of a traditional religion, because it is the individual's (Leo) personal creative energy that matters. The Age of Pisces is over.

The age of flight is also part of this new Age. We have gone from walking on the ground to walking on the moon in the last 100+ years. The popularity of *Star Wars* reflects the seeds of this new Age of Aquarius. An Air sign, Aquarius rules flight, unfettered communication, freedom, invention, the unusual, and acceptance of people from all walks and backgrounds.

The Statue of Liberty would appear to straddle both the Piscean and Aquarian Ages ... with its torch of "light" leading the way for the huddled masses to move forward into a new age of enlightenment and recognition of the creativity that each person has to contribute to society.

With this Age of Aquarius, we must pay heed to the line by Lawrence Alexander from his novel *Rubicon*, mentioned at the beginning of this book: we must not make "the mistake in thinking that the aim of intelligence is the expansion of knowledge rather than the depth of understanding." In this new Age of Aquarius, information (knowledge) is expanding. We have bits of information instantaneously at our hands about everything, but are we losing the capacity to understand any one subject deeply? Food for thought.

Sidereal vs. Tropical Astrology:
Some astrologers practice what is called Sidereal Astrology. This technique uses the constellations as a backdrop. Because the vernal equinox moves backward through the constellations one degree every 72 years (the Precession of the Equinoxes), their system is different from the Tropical Zodiac that many Western astrologers use today.

Tropical Astrology relates to life here on Earth. Referencing the Sun's flow between the Tropic of Cancer and the Tropic of Capricorn, which creates the seasons, this makes sense because we live our lives according to the seasons on this planet—not because of the influence of the loosely knit and overlapping constellations. In the spring, we plant; in the summer, we eat some of our produce and tend those that will take us through the winter; in the fall, we harvest those winter crops; and in the winter, we hunker down, rest, share, and wait for spring. This scenario, of course, doesn't apply to every location on the planet, and is reversed south of the equator, but it is the basic pattern of the life cycle.

Tropical Astrology was adopted during the Hellenistic Period, around 323 BCE. At that time, the astrologers named the first point of spring on the earth as zero degrees Aries (only because at that time the Spring Equinox happened to line up with the constellation Aries). They used zero degrees of Aries as the starting point of the zodiac each year. They were not talking about the constellation Aries; they were talking about the moment of spring when the sun crosses the equator going north, the Vernal Equinox. Tropical Astrology has nothing to do with the constellations.

Let me say that again: Tropical Astrology we use has nothing to do with the constellations.

Every year at the exact moment of the Vernal Equinox, the Tropical Zodiac is set up with 0 degrees of Aries as the starting point.

In the book, *Larousse Encyclopedia of Astrology*, the entry under Tropical Zodiac reads: "the signs Aries through Pisces ... derive a good deal of their meaning from the seasons ... at least in the Northern Hemisphere ... the constellations themselves are arbitrary, subjectively perceived patterns of stars physically unrelated to one another ... they do not have definite boundaries ... They overlap and are greatly varying in size and shape." (Contributing editors astrologers Rob Hand, Charles Harvey, and Charles Jayne, p.292)

And in that same book, under the entry Sidereal Zodiac, it reads: "the sidereal zodiac has no obvious starting point..." (p.255)

Bruce Scofield in his article titled "The Zodiac: Sidereal vs. Tropical," originally published in *The Mountain Astrologer*, 2001, quoted the twentieth century renowned astrologer Dane Rudhyar: "the sidereal zodiac, the zodiac of constellations, was the product of the myth-making faculty of the human psyche." Rudhyar saw the tropical zodiac as the proper framework on which to assess the evolution of mankind. (Rudhyar, Dane. *Birth Patterns for a New Humanity*. The Netherlands: Servire-Wassenaar. 1969. pp. 85 ff.) Note: this book was later reprinted under the title *Astrological Timing*.

Ephemeris, Plural Ephemerides:
An ephemeris is a book that lists the planets in their signs every day, as well as the new and full moons, eclipses, and more. Some ephemerides cover 100 years; some cover fifty years. Midnight and Noontime editions are available. I prefer the Midnight edition because it covers the entire day, whereas the Noon edition starts in the middle of the day.

The Astrological Rulership Book
For a list of entries that are categorized separately by the planets, the signs, and the houses, find a copy of Rex Bill's *Rulership Book*. It may be out of print, but it's worth the effort. This book is an excellent source when you want to know what rules rashes, in what house you can find mushrooms, or where your Uncle Harry or great aunt Gertrude have hidden the family jewels ... or maybe you don't want to know that ... regardless, the book will come in handy, believe me.

That's all, folks! I'm sure, once this manuscript leaves my hands, I'll think of more things I should have said. But that is the nature of life ... learning new things every day.

Let the sky be your limit!

Endnotes

Chapter 1:

1. Yes, Pluto is still a planet in astrology, and remains such in the minds of many astronomers and certainly all astrologers as we have witnessed the repercussions of Pluto, since its discovery over eighty-five years ago, on this planet and certainly in individual lives. On August 24, 2006, on the last day of the International Astronomical Union conference in Prague, a handful of the remaining astronomers voted to demote Pluto to a dwarf planet. "I'm embarrassed for astronomy," said Alan Stern, leader of NASA's New Horizon's mission to Pluto and a scientist at the Southwest Research Institute. "Less than five percent of the world's astronomers voted." He expects the astronomical community to overturn the decision. (www.space.com/2791-pluto-demoted-longer-planet-highly-controversial-definition.html)

Chapter 10:

1. The Greco/Egyptian astrologer, mathematician, and astronomer, Claudius Ptolemy (second century ACE) authored *Tetrabiblos*, one of the oldest complete books on astrology that answered the scientific and religious critics of his day. In his book he recognized only five aspects: conjunction, sextile, square, trine, and opposition. These five aspects are referred to as the Ptolemaic aspects, sometimes called the "major aspects."

....

List of Astrological Resources

As of February 2017, the following information is up to date.

For a copy of your chart, please contact Dusty at:
dustybunker@comcast.net
www.dustybunker.com

You can also receive a copy of your chart from my colleague:
Dorothy Morgan at
nhastrologer@gmail.com
www.nhastrologer.com

Also For charts and services:

Astro Computing Services
68 A Fogg Road
Epping, NH 03042
(603) 743-4300
Maria Kay Simms
www.astrocom.com

Organizations:

National Council for Geocosmic Research, Inc. (NCGR)
www.geocosmic.org

> They have a "how to contact us" link on their website.
> Also, a list of Officers, Director, and Staff with email addresses

Association For Astrological Networking (AFAN)
www.afan.org

> Their statement: We enhance, protect, and validate the important role astrologers and astrology have in today's society.

Publications:

The Mountain Astrologer (TMA)
P. O. Box 970
Cedar Ridge, CA 95924
www.mountainastrologer.com

Dell Horoscope Magazine
267 Broadway
4th floor
New York, NY 10007
(212) 686-7188

> On occasion, their monthly issue will list the astrological associations in each state who have monthly meetings. Contact them for the one closest to you. They can also direct you to an astrologer.

For astrological software:

Astrolabe Inc.
P. O. Box 1750
Brewster, MA 02631
www.alabe.com

....

Bibliography

Alexander, Lawrence. *Rubicon.* Harper Collins Publishers. New York, 2008.
Byron, George Gordon. Lord Byron. *The Corsair.* John. Murray. 1814.
Frost, Robert. *The Secret Sits.* 1945. www.internal.org/Robert_Frost
Gibran, Kahlil. *The Prophet.* Alfred A. Knopf, Inc. 1923
Larousse Encyclopedia of Astrology. New American Library. 1977.
Scofield. *The Zodiac: Sidereal vs. Tropical.* The Mountain Astrologer. 2001.
Wallace, William Ross. *What Rules the World.* Wilson & Fiske. 1891.

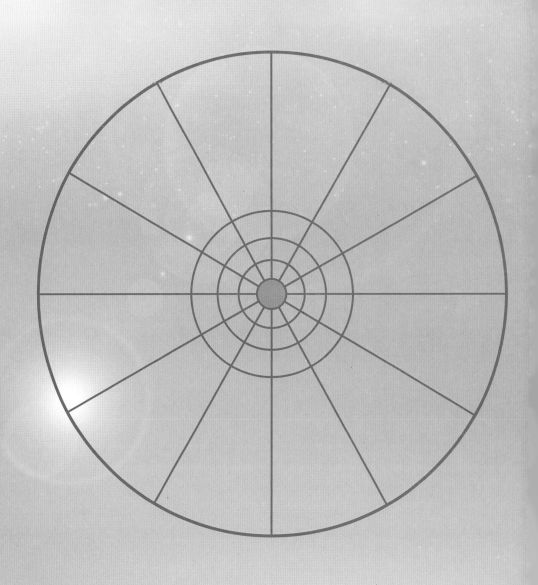